Assessing Students' Learning

James H. McMillan, *Editor*
Virginia Commonwealth University

NEW DIRECTIONS FOR TEACHING AND LEARNING

ROBERT E. YOUNG, *Editor-in-Chief*
University of Wisconsin

KENNETH E. EBLE, *Consulting Editor*
University of Utah, Salt Lake City

Number 34, Summer 1988

Paperback sourcebooks in
The Jossey-Bass Higher Education Series

Jossey-Bass Inc., Publishers
San Francisco • London

James H. McMillan (ed.).
Assessing Students' Learning.
New Directions for Teaching and Learning, no. 34.
San Francisco: Jossey-Bass, 1988.

New Directions for Teaching and Learning
Robert E. Young, *Editor-in-Chief*
Kenneth E. Eble, *Consulting Editor*

New Directions for Teaching and Learning is published quarterly
by Jossey-Bass Inc., Publishers, 350 Sansome Street, San Francisco,
California, 94104. Application to mail at second-class postage rates
is pending at San Francisco, California, and at additional mailing
offices. POSTMASTER: Send address changes to *New Directions for
Teaching and Learning*, Jossey-Bass Inc., Publishers, 350 Sansome
Street, San Francisco, California 94104.

Editorial correspondence should be sent to the Editor-in-Chief,
Robert E. Young, Dean, University of Wisconsin Center, Fox Valley,
1478 Midway Rd., Menasha, Wisconsin 54952.

Library of Congress Catalog Card Number LC 85-644763

International Standard Serial Number ISSN 0271-0633

International Standard Book Number ISBN 1-55542-929-7

Cover art by WILLI BAUM

Manufactured in the United States of America

Ordering Information

The paperback sourcebooks listed below are published quarterly and can be ordered either by subscription or single copy.

Subscriptions cost $48.00 per year for institutions, agencies, and libraries. Individuals can subscribe at the special rate of $36.00 per year *if payment is by personal check*. (Note that the full rate of $48.00 applies if payment is by institutional check, even if the subscription is designated for an individual.) Standing orders are accepted.

Single copies are available at $11.95 when payment accompanies order. (California, New Jersey, New York, and Washington, D.C., residents please include appropriate sales tax.) For billed orders, cost per copy is $11.95 plus postage and handling.

Substantial discounts are offered to organizations and individuals wishing to purchase bulk quantities of Jossey-Bass sourcebooks. Please inquire.

Please note that these prices are for the calendar year 1988 and are subject to change without notice. Also, some titles may be out of print and therefore not available for sale.

To ensure correct and prompt delivery, all orders must give either the *name of an individual* or an *official purchase order number*. Please submit your order as follows:

Subscriptions: specify series and year subscription is to begin.
Single Copies: specify sourcebook code (such as, TL1) and first two words of title.

Mail orders for United States and Possessions, Latin America, Canada, Japan, Australia, and New Zealand to:
Jossey-Bass Inc., Publishers
350 Sansome Street
San Francisco, California 94104

Mail orders for all other parts of the world to:
Jossey-Bass Limited
28 Banner Street
London EC1Y 8QE

New Directions for Teaching and Learning Series
Robert E. Young, *Editor-in-Chief*
Kenneth E. Eble, *Consulting Editor*

Contents

Editor's Notes

Fueled by recent national reports, there is a growing concern about the quality of higher education. One response to this concern has been a greater emphasis on institutional accountability through measuring student outcomes—what has now become the assessment movement in higher education. Indeed, assessment has established itself as more than a passing fad; it is likely to have pervasive and long-lasting effects. There have been numerous conferences and publications focused on assessment, and most agree that in substance, if not in name, assessment of some form will constitute an important aspect of higher education.

But what is so new? Faculty have always assessed student learning, using descriptors such as *testing, measuring,* or *evaluating.* Assessment is an integral part of the teaching-learning process. Because much of the pressure for increased assessment has come from outside the academy—from the public, state government, and accrediting bodies—the current emphasis is on using assessment for institutional accountability. The result is that assessment is an "add-on," for most institutions. Often it is implemented as a centrally coordinated effort that requires students to take additional tests or complete sets of questionnaires. An office for student assessment may be established in which external funds are used to initiate institutionwide assessment programs. But when assessment is an "add-on" it is outside the normal teaching-learning process. There is little incentive for faculty to become involved, and the focus is rarely on individual student learning. Rather, the emphasis is typically on broad, general outcomes (for example, general education), results of large groups of students, and program evaluation. It consists essentially of an additional set of requirements, and in most institutions that means taking resources away from other programs. Perhaps this is why Cross (1987) has said, "Despite all of the current enthusiasm for assessment, it looks as though it will stop short of the classroom door, doing little to improve the quality of learning in the average classroom" (p. 5).

This sourcebook has a different focus, viewing effective assessment as an inside-out activity. Since assessment is an integral aspect of the teaching-learning process, it is an essential part of what is done by faculty in each course and department. There may be a need to establish institutionwide learning objectives, but it is argued that the evaluation of learning outcomes is best achieved by assessment in established, ongoing courses by individual faculty. Assessment is most effective when it is conceived, discussed, and implemented by faculty in their classes. Thus the purpose of this volume is to present assessment strategies and infor-

1

mation, based on recent research and practical experience, to provide new assessment ideas and approaches that emphasize student learning and effective teaching. Indeed, it could be argued that some dimensions of institutional effectiveness can be thought of as the cumulative effect of individual courses and departments—to help faculty improve what they already do.

Fundamental principles of assessment are presented in the first two chapters. Jon F. Wergin provides a provocative discussion in Chapter One of important issues that are basic to any type of assessment, including the trade-off between control and relevance of the test, the fit between course objectives and test items, characteristics of norm-referenced and criterion-referenced assessments, the "objectivity" myth, a new definition of test validity, error in testing and reliability (yes, even the best assessments include errors), and the importance of test analysis. In Chapter Two, Georgine Loacker draws on extensive experience in assessment at Alverno College to present the fundamental parts of assessment as an integrated whole: deciding what is to be assessed, identifying criteria and instrumentation, implementing assessment approaches, interpreting results, and giving feedback. Several benefits of effective assessment are also presented: Clarifying what should be taught, refining expectations about college-level learning, involving students in the learning process, adapting pedagogy, providing feedback about instructional strategies, bringing about collaboration of faculty, and the renewing of faculty teaching practice. Loacker argues convincingly for greater faculty involvement in the assessment process.

The next four chapters present strategies and recommendations for assessing specific skills or areas. Two skills that have been emphasized recently are critical thinking and writing. These skills, often articulated in the form of institutionwide objectives or goals, are developed in the context of individual courses. C. Blaine Carpenter and James C. Doig, who have been involved in teaching and assessing critical thinking across the curriculum, point out in Chapter Three that the first step in measuring critical thinking is to identify critical thinking in the context of specific courses and programs. This may be the most difficult step. Once a conception is found, approaches to assessment can be matched to that aspect of student learning. Current approaches to assessing critical thinking are summarized, including standardized tests, locally devised instruments, and those utilized by different institutions.

The importance of assessing writing in each course is stressed by Karen L. Greenberg in Chapter Four. Writing is a skill that can be used to improve learning, particularly the acquisition and practice of higher-order thinking skills. In this chapter, techniques for assessing writing across the curriculum are presented, with suggestions for how writing assignments can be used to assess students' mastery of content.

The role of faculty judgments about learning outcomes, criteria, standards, and documentation in the assessment of students' prior learning is emphasized in Chapter Five by Susan Simosko. Experiential learning occurs when job or life experience leads to competence in a particular skill or domain of knowledge. The assessment of experiential learning is becoming more important as adult students bring rich experiences to the college classroom. This chapter summarizes procedures used to assess experiential learning.

Bobby Fong shows in Chapter Six how assessing the major can be accomplished to support and enhance teaching and learning. The techniques reviewed include using commercially designed examinations, theses and projects, orals, comprehensives, portfolios, and external examiners. Since assessment of the major is embedded in a department's philosophy of teaching and learning, it is an effective means of evaluating the impact of a curriculum on students. Fong argues that a necessary step in this kind of assessment is for faculty to define the rationale and content of their major programs to develop a clear statement of what faculty expect students to achieve.

Chapter Seven is an innovative discussion by Howard R. Pollio and W. Lee Humphreys of an old topic—grading. Grades and grading are integral to the assessment process, and the manner in which grades are used affects the academic climate of teaching and learning. Research and knowledge about grading are used to identify important implications for assessment, and recommendations are made to improve the use of grades and grading to enhance teaching and learning.

Each of the chapters contain important principles for improving student assessment and, ultimately, the quality of teaching and learning. The emphasis is on evaluation at the level of classrooms by individual faculty, using current theory and research on assessment, as well as specific examples of how assessment can be improved.

James H. McMillan
Editor

Reference

Cross, K. P. "Teaching for Learning." *American Association for Higher Education Bulletin*, 1987, *39* (8), 3–7.

James H. McMillan is associate professor of educational studies at Virginia Commonwealth University in Richmond. His interests are the development of critical thinking and values in college students and the assessment of educational outcomes.

Attention to certain basic principles that are frequently overlooked in classroom tests can significantly enhance student learning.

Basic Issues and Principles in Classroom Assessment

Jon F. Wergin

If we have learned anything from educational research over the last fifty years, it is that students learn according to how they are tested. If we test students for factual recall, then they will memorize a set of facts. If we test them for their ability to analyze relationships, then they will begin to learn to think critically. If we assess how well they can apply classroom material to concrete problems, then they will learn to do that. But despite the general agreement that classroom assessment procedures have a powerful influence over student learning, testing is the bane of most faculty members' lives. If college teaching is the only profession for which its members are never formally trained, then the way in which faculty evaluate students is perhaps the most glaring example of that deficit. We all have personal horror stories of how inappropriate, even grotesque, college exams can be. Mine is based on a one-item final exam from an undergraduate social psychology course I took about twenty years ago: "Discuss the history of social psychology in the twentieth century, including all relevant names and dates."

National, standardized tests (such as the Graduate Record Examination or the tests of the National Board of Medical Examiners) have become quite sophisticated in recent years, with impressive psychometric credentials; yet most of the over 100 million tests given annually in higher

J. H. McMillan (ed.). *Assessing Students' Learning.*
New Directions for Teaching and Learning, no. 34. San Francisco: Jossey-Bass, Summer 1988.

education are put together by classroom teachers, and as McKee and Manning-Curtis (1982) point out, a college student's grade point average depends almost entirely on such measures. Even though calls for greater accountability in higher education have made *assessment* one of the educational buzzwords of the 1980s, and even though colleges and universities are responding to this pressure by placing more emphasis on institutionwide evaluations of student outcomes, the major responsibility for measuring student performance will likely remain with the individual classroom teacher.

The purpose of this chapter is to outline and discuss some general principles faculty members can use to improve their assessment procedures, short of converting themselves into professional psychometricians. The chapter has three parts. First is a discussion of three basic issues in student assessment: the concern for control versus relevance, the use of so-called norm- versus criterion-referenced measures, and the emphasis on what I am calling the objectivity myth. Next comes a discussion of two key concepts in educational measurement, validity and reliability. The chapter concludes with some thoughts about how assessment data can be analyzed and used to help improve student learning.

Basic Issues in Student Assessment

Control Versus Relevance. Probably the most vexing and important problem facing any test developer, whether that person is a classroom teacher or a specialist at the Educational Testing Service, is how to maximize two criteria. The first is control—ensuring comparability across students by having them respond to the same test stimuli and by assessing those responses equally and fairly. The second is relevance—ensuring congruence between skills required to perform well on the test and knowledge or skills required to accomplish course objectives. The problem is that, desirable as both criteria may be, they tend to be almost mutually exclusive; that is, tests high in control tend to be low in relevance, and vice versa (see Figure 1).

Typical classroom tests are represented on the left of the figure. They are high on the control criterion (all students respond to the same set of test items, and everyone is graded in the same way), but their relevance is low (very few real-life situations require the ability to answer

Figure 1. Characteristics of Classroom Assessments

High	⟵—————————	*Control*	—————————⟶	Low
Low	⟵—————————	*Relevance*	—————————⟶	High

| *"Objective" tests* (multiple-choice, true-false, etc.) | *Essay tests* | *Simulations* | *Performance tests* |

multiple-choice questions). Further, because objective tests are very diffi-cult and time consuming to construct well, they tend to favor simple recall of facts. Essay tests are more relevant, as students can be tested for their understanding of complex relationships and their ability to express themselves, but these tests sacrifice some control; grader error can seriously affect the accuracy and consistency of the scoring procedure. At the other end of the scale are performance tests (for example, observation ratings of student teachers). These score high on the relevance criterion, as they directly measure the skills being taught, but the control of these assessments is notoriously low. Natural work environments are not easily manipulated and defy standardization; thus, the test stimuli can vary greatly. Moreover, ratings tend to be highly influenced by various forms of rater bias, such as the halo effect (rating a specific skill on the basis of an overall impression), the contrast effect (using oneself, rather than external criteria, as the standard of comparison), and the error of leniency (giving the student the benefit of the doubt on skills inadequately observed) (Guilford, 1954).

In recent years, interest in simulations has grown as a possible com-promise between the twin desiderata of control and relevance. First intro-duced as pencil-and-paper exercises, and evolving later into sophisticated computerized problems, simulations typically put the student into a real-istic problem situation requiring a series of decisions. In so-called branched simulations, each decision is contingent on what the student has done so far. A medical student may be asked to handle an emergency-room patient, for example, or an engineering student may be asked to work through a problem in the design of a highway overpass. The premise behind simulations is an intriguing one: to put the student into a situa-tion that is both standardized and professionally relevant. Some national certifying bodies, such as the National Board of Medical Examiners, have developed and used simulations extensively in their own examinations, but this technique also has its problems. Critics have asserted that simula-tions measure only a narrow range of skills, are relevant only in superficial ways, and do not accurately predict professional performance (Norcini and Swanson, 1988). In short, while simulations offer the benefit of measures high in both relevance and control, they also suffer from both kinds of deficits. The development cost of good simulations also puts them out of reach for many routine classroom applications.

Still, the thinking that has gone into simulations is useful for the college teacher. The question is "How can I make my classroom assess-ments more relevant to what I want the students to learn, without sacri-ficing control?" The assessment method selected should fit what is being taught as closely as possible. If it is mastery of information, relevance may be less important than control; if it is acquisition of skill at solving problems, the reverse may be true.

Norm-Referenced Versus Criterion-Referenced Tests. A second basic issue is the purpose of assessment. Is it to distribute students on a scale of ability or knowledge, from most to least? This would result in what is known as a norm-referenced test. Or is the purpose to judge whether students have completed the course objectives satisfactorily? This would imply the use of a criterion-referenced test. The difference is not inconsequential, since the two perspectives are based on quite different assumptions about the nature of the measurement and the purpose for which it will be used. Suppose, as the parent of eight-year-old Johnny, you were to ask Johnny's teacher how he was doing in school. Which of the following responses would be most helpful?

> Johnny has mastered the third-grade readings and is an active participant in class. His spelling and penmanship could stand improvement, though.

> Johnny is near the top of his class in reading and class participation, but below average in spelling and penmanship.

Interpretation of the first response requires an understanding of the criteria used by the teacher in making her judgments. Interpretation of the second requires understanding of the characteristics of the class (the "norm"). The basic differences between the two purposes of assessment are captured in Table 1.

Norm-referenced measures are based on classical test theory, which assumes that the best test is one that produces a normal (bell-shaped) distribution of responses and maximizes the distance among examinees. The test itself is assumed to be a random sample from a large domain of content. Standardized examinations such as the ACT, the SAT, and the GRE are all examples of norm-referenced measures, as are classroom tests graded "on the curve."

Criterion-referenced measures are based more on intuitive than on statistical logic. Here the assumption is that the best test communicates how well the student has mastered a set of very specific objectives; thus, a

Table 1. Comparison of Norm- and Criterion-Referenced Measurement

	NRM	CRM
Purpose:	discrimination/selection	diagnosis/mastery
Source of items:	general objectives	specific objectives
Test composition:	sample from large pool of items	complete coverage of objectives
Scores:	variability desirable	variability irrelevant
Interpretation:	relative standing	what student can do

normal distribution of scores is not important or even desirable, since the instructional goal is maximum learning rather than maximum discrimination. Students compete against a set of standards, not against one another.

One rule to follow is this: If the instructional goals are general, complete mastery of the educational domain is unrealistic, and if the ultimate purpose is to select the best and the brightest, consider using a norm-referenced approach; if the goals are quite specific, or if the ultimate purpose is to ensure that students have mastered certain competencies, consider the criterion-referenced approach (Hanna and Cashin, 1987).

The Objectivity Myth. The debate about how objective tests should be has been going on for most of this century (Milton, 1982). Multiple-choice items were invented during World War I to process large numbers of new soldiers and as a reaction to the subjectivity (read "error") observed in the grading of essay questions. These new tests, because they were all scored the same no matter who did the scoring, became known as objective tests. Thus, objective tests were supposedly free of bias, while subjective tests were to be avoided.

Such unfortunate illogic has persisted to this day. It may be traced to what Scriven (1972) has called a fundamental confusion between two quite different meanings of the objective-subjective dimension. In the first of these meanings, objectivity and subjectivity are contrasted in a quantitative sense: *Subjective* refers to what one person experiences, while *objective* refers to what a number of people experience. The second sense, however, contrasts the two terms in a qualitative sense—namely, the quality of the evidence presented. Here, *subjective* refers to personal opinion, probably biased, while *objective* refers to verifiable truth. As Scriven points out, "It would certainly be delightful if these two senses coincided, so that all reports of personal experience, for example, were less reliable than all reports of events witnessed by a large number of people. But as one thinks of the reliability of reports about felt pain or perceived size, on the one hand, and the reports about the achievements of stage magicians or mentalists on the other, we would not find this coincidence impressive" (1972, p. 95).

Still, the tendency to equate the two meanings has been a powerful one in the history of educational measurement. Objectivity, in the qualitative sense, is assumed to be achieved through attaining objectivity in the quantitative sense; and the latter is accomplished, so the logic goes, by the development of tests that are all scored the same way. Give the scoring key for a multiple-choice test to a set of ten graders, and all ten will produce the same scores virtually every time. This logic has only been strengthened by the development of computerized scoring procedures, which crank out impressive-looking statistics. Qualitative judgment becomes buried under the numbers.

The fallacy, of course, is the assumption that test bias can be eliminated through enhancement of quantitative objectivity. One has only to consider the massive research on standardized test bias against minority populations (Wigdor and Garner, 1982; Reynolds and Brown, 1984), or the development of an entire generation of sophisticated test takers who are unable to write a coherent paragraph, for confirmation of how pervasive this fallacy has been. The fact is that all tests are vulnerable to bias and unfairness. A sloppily constructed multiple-choice test can result in a score just as capricious and arbitrary as a poorly graded essay exam. I agree with Milton's (1982) assertion that the term *objective* should be banned from the measurement lexicon. In his words, "All classroom tests are subjective in one way or another. To seek objective evaluations about students is a waste of time—there are no such things . . . " (p. 22). (I will continue to use the word *objective* in this chapter to refer to a certain type of test item, but only because the word is still commonly used that way; here, it will appear within quotation marks.) Thus, the objective-subjective issue is misleading. The real question is how to minimize interpretive error, and the answer requires a brief discussion of two measurement concepts, validity and reliability.

Test Validity

The *Standards for Educational and Psychological Testing* (Joint Committee, 1985) state "validity" as "the most important consideration in test evaluation. . . . The concept refers to the appropriateness, meaningfulness, and usefulness of the specific inferences made from test scores" (p. 9). The validity of a classroom test is the extent to which test scores allow the instructor to infer how well students have attained course aims or objectives. While there are several different types of validity evidence, two are most important for classroom tests.

Content Validity Evidence. Content validity is the extent to which a test adequately samples course content and objectives. One of the most common student complaints about tests is that they measure trivial information not reflective of material stressed in the course. The best way to enhance the content validity of a test is to begin with a test blueprint, sometimes called a table of specifications (Gronlund, 1977). It is nothing more than a simple matrix, listing on one dimension topic areas to be covered, and on the other skills or objectives to be assessed. Consider the sample blueprint shown in Figure 2 for a course in classroom testing. Four topics are to be covered on the test; four levels of skill are to be measured. The first step is to determine how much weight each topic is to have. The example shows that 15 percent of the test should cover assessment planning. The next step is to partition each percentage across objectives or skill levels. In the example above, therefore, 20 percent of

Figure 2. A Test Blueprint

Content	Recall	Skills Application	Analysis	Synthesis
Assessment planning: 15%	5	10		
Psychometric principles: 30%	20	5	5	
Item writing: 35%	10			25
Test analysis: 20%	5	10	5	

the test should deal with recall of psychometric principles, while 25 percent should require the student to write test items.

A test blueprint can help the test developer avoid one of the most common traps in classroom assessment: setting out to measure higher-order thinking (such as analysis or synthesis), but actually measuring only rote memorization. Milton (1982) reports on a number of studies of classroom test content, all of which reveal that most test questions require a knowledge of facts and little more, despite stated course objectives. The reason is fairly obvious: Factual items are relatively easy to write and grade; measuring analysis or problem solving is very difficult, especially in a multiple-choice format. A test blueprint keeps the test maker honest.

Construct Validity Evidence. Construct validity is the extent to which a test measures the amount learned, and not some other extraneous variable. The most serious threat to construct validity in "objective" tests are poorly worded items that measure test-taking skill, rather than mastery of the material. Consider these examples:

1. Chronic nutritional cirrhosis is characterized by all of the following *except:*
   a. ascites
   b. palmar erythema
   c. jaundice
   d. liver edge 6 cm. below the diaphram
   e. esophageal varices
2. Maintaining the chain of possession is of the utmost importance to preserve the integrity of physical evidence. This statement means:
   a. having a supervisory officer witness the marking of evidence to assure its future identification
   b. having command personnel review and initial all inventory reports
   c. accounting for every person who has handled the evidence
   d. placing all evidence linking a subject to a crime into one specially sterilized container
3. Psychologists who use such terms as *reinforcement, conditioning,* and *discriminative stimuli* are called:

a. cognitive
b. psychodynamic
c. behaviorists
d. clinical

A testwise person should be able to answer all three items correctly, even if he or she knows nothing about medicine, criminal justice, or psychology. In the first case the correct answer, *d,* is longer and more detailed than the others; in the second, the correct answer, *c,* is the only one that logically fits with the phrase "chain of possession"; in the third, only option *c,* is grammatically consistent with the item stem. These are three of the most common errors in item writing (Millman, Bishop, and Ebel, 1965).

The most serious threat to construct validity in essay tests is in scoring—grading on the basis of neatness or penmanship, for example, when these criteria are not part of course objectives, or grading on the basis of an overall image of the student (the halo effect).

Test Reliability

The Joint Committee (1985) defines *reliability* as "the degree to which test scores are free from errors of measurement" (p. 19). Numerous factors can influence measurement error, including student fatigue, item sampling, and student guessing. Characteristics of the test itself will also affect reliability. As with validity, the major threats to reliability in "objective" tests are in item construction. Consider these examples:

1. The fluid used to aid the cohesiveness of powders for hypodermic tablets is:
   a. alcohol
   b. syrup
   c. PVP in 50% alcohol
   d. distilled water
   e. none of these
2. *(true or false)* The nourishment assimilated by the body depends on the amount of food eaten.
3. *Huckleberry Finn* was written by _____ .

For item 1, the correct answer should be "50 percent alcohol *solution,*" so technically the correct response is *e* ("none of these"). Students who know the material may pick *a,* however, assuming that the term *solution* is implicit in the answer. Item 2 is ambiguous, and may be either true or false, depending on how the intent of the item is interpreted. And in item 3, the answer, "Mark Twain," seems obvious, but the question is phrased in such a way that numerous *other* answers are technically correct—"Samuel Clemens," "1910," "a man," and "hand," to name just a few. In addition to trick questions and ambiguous wording, the length of the test can also affect reliability. Very short tests risk an undersampling of course content, while very long tests risk learner fatigue.

For essay tests, reliability is most affected by grader variability in scoring: grader fatigue, order of grading (pity the poor student whose paper falls immediately behind the best one in the class), and inconsistent application of grading standards. As noted earlier, observed unreliability of essay grading was what originally led to the development of "objective" test forms. Through the years the conventional wisdom has been that, bad as essay tests are, the instructor needs at the very least to grade essay responses using a specific set of criteria, with differential weights assigned to each criterion. But about twenty years ago the Educational Testing Service developed something called *holistic scoring* as a method of evaluating writing samples. It is based on the commonsense belief that assessing the total effect of written discourse can be more important than simply adding up subscores on such factors as clarity, syntax, and organization; instead, the work is judged as a whole. With careful training, discussion, and feedback among raters, holistic scoring can be remarkably reliable (Conlan, 1978). This is an example of how a truly subjective assessment is not also inherently biased. It is both subjective, in the quantitative sense, and objective, in the qualitative sense.

Probably the single best way to improve reliability in classroom assessment is to use multiple measures. This can be done both by testing students frequently and by using various test formats. For example, several short tests employing a variety of test items are likely to be more reliable than one or two major exams consisting entirely of multiple-choice questions.

Test Analysis

Most people assume that analysis of a test can be done only after the fact, when student performance data have been generated. To make this assumption is to neglect what might be called the ounce-of-prevention principle, which suggests that devoting one hour to a colleague's review of the exam is better than devoting five hours answering students' challenges. In a survey undertaken several years ago, McKee and Manning-Curtis (1982) found that colleague review was one of the testing practices least used by college faculty. Colleague review can be helpful in at least four ways. First, a colleague can review test content for congruence with the test blueprint. Do items reflect the specified topic weights? More important, do the items measure the range of skills or abilities specified? Second, a faculty colleague can look for ambiguities in item phrasing. Are the directions unclear? Is the language vague or confusing? Third, if the test employs multiple-choice items, a colleague can check for response options that are ambiguous, obviously correct or incorrect, or misleading (college faculty tend to be quite testwise themselves and are thus able to spot obvious cues). Fourth, if the test employs essay questions, colleagues can review the scoring criteria for accuracy, specificity, and emphasis.

The appropriate post hoc analysis will depend on the type of test items used. For "objective" tests, since the predominant threats to validity and reliability occur during item *construction,* the major questions are the following.

1. Was the item too difficult or too easy? Determination of appropriate item difficulty depends on whether the test has a norm-referenced or a criterion-referenced focus. For norm-referenced tests, the average item difficulty should hover around 50 percent (that is 50 percent of the students answer the item correctly) (Ebel, 1979); item difficulties substantially above or below that figure do not discriminate well (see question 2). For criterion-referenced tests, the standard is quite different. Appropriate item difficulty depends on whether the course objective measured by the item is one for which mastery is expected. In that case, item difficulties substantially below 100 percent should be examined carefully.

2. Did students who received high total scores get the items right? This is known as the item's *discrimination* power (Gronlund, 1977). For norm-referenced tests, good items are those that are answered correctly by students with high total scores and answered incorrectly by students with low total scores. By definition, discrimination power does not apply to criterion-referenced tests and may in fact indicate an inappropriate item. Nevertheless, any item that shows negative discrimination (that is, favoring low-scoring students) almost always needs revision, regardless of test purpose, since for some reason the better students were drawn to the wrong answer in disproportionate numbers.

3. For multiple-choice tests, were the distractors (wrong answers) effective as distractors? Wrong answers that fail to attract any responses are a waste of space and reading time; conversely, distractors that attract a disproportionately high response may be open to challenge as technically correct or at least misleading.

For essay tests, since the predominant threats to validity and reliability occur in *scoring,* the major questions are these.

1. How accurately were the scoring criteria applied? Using a cograder for at least a sample of papers provides a measure of systematic bias, and analyzing discrepancies helps to make the grading criteria more explicit. This is especially important with holistic grading procedures.

2. How stable was the grader across responses? Grader fatigue represents a significant threat to reliability; thus, regrading a small sample of papers in a different order and at another time provides a rough stability index.

Summary and Conclusions

Boyer (1987) states, "In the end, excellence in education will be achieved not simply through better testing but through better teaching" (p. 262). Of course, test quality is important. A classroom test that is seriously lacking in validity or reliability is worse than useless; it provides misleading and potentially harmful information. But a larger question is how classroom tests can lead to improved teaching and learning. Such a result is more likely when:

1. *Assessments are maximally relevant to the skills being taught.* Avoid measuring complex behaviors (such as critical thinking) with true-false questions. Make the assessment task into an opportunity for students to practice what you are trying to teach them.

2. *Assessments give students information about what they know or can do.* Usually this means adopting a criterion-referenced philosophy about testing. It also means giving students an opportunity to revise their work on the basis of careful and concise feedback, as well as accepting the notion that "the ideal end product is a population of students who have *all* finally passed because they have been given enough time to help to do what we ask of them" (Elbow and Belanoff, 1986, p. 337).

These considerations are difficult but not impossible to satisfy. Many creative approaches are possible, even with traditional test formats. German (1984), for example, has tested students' mastery of theoretical material in a public-speaking course by presenting them with videotaped speeches and a corresponding set of multiple-choice questions, which are then reviewed after the exam. In my own courses on research methods, I have asked students to write grant proposals, which are then rated by other members of the class. Elbow and his colleagues at SUNY–Stony Brook replaced the usual examinations in English with student portfolios, sets of revised compositions put together by a student and graded by faculty other than the student's own instructor (Elbow and Belanoff, 1986).

Are such systems as these time consuming? Yes, perhaps, especially at first, when the bugs are being worked out. The incentives are mostly intrinsic, but instructors who have experienced the positive impact of improved assessment in their classrooms realize just how powerful such incentives can be.

Additional Readings

Conceptual/Technical Issues

Burns, E. *The Development, Use and Abuse of Educational Tests.* Springfield, Ill.: Thomas, 1979.

16

Ebel, R. L., and Frisbie, D. A. *Essentials of Educational Measurement.* (4th ed.) Englewood Cliffs, N.J.: Prentice-Hall, 1986.

Gronlund, N. E. *Measurement and Evaluation in Education and Psychology.* (3rd ed.) New York: Holt, Rinehart & Winston, 1984.

Guskey, T. R. *Implementing Mastery Teaching.* Belmont, Calif.: Wadsworth, 1985.

Mehrens, W. A., and Lehmann, I. J. *Measurement and Evaluation in Education and Psychology.* (3rd ed.) New York: Holt, Rinehart & Winston, 1984.

Plake, B. S. (ed.). *Social and Technical Issues in Testing: Implications for Test Construction and Usage.* Hillsdale, N.J.: Erlbaum, 1984.

Popham, W. J. *Criterion-Referenced Measurement.* Englewood Cliffs, N.J.: Prentice-Hall, 1978.

Tyler, R. W., and Wolf, R. M. *Crucial Issues in Testing.* Berkeley, Calif.: McCutchan, 1974.

Practical Tips

Brossell, G. "Essay Test Topic Development." Paper presented at the annual meeting of the Conference on Writing Assessment, Cleveland, Ohio, 1986. (ED 279 002)

Cashin, W. E. *Improving Essay Tests.* IDEA paper no. 17. Manhattan: Center for Faculty Evaluation and Development, Kansas State University, 1987.

Clegg, V. L., and Cashin, W. E. *Improving Multiple Choice Tests.* IDEA paper no. 16. Manhattan: Center for Faculty Evaluation and Development, Kansas State University, 1986.

Dolly, J. P., and Williams, K. S. "Teaching Testwiseness." Paper presented at the annual meeting of the Rocky Mountain Educational Research Association, 1983. (ED 241 562)

McKeachie, W. J. *Teaching Tips: A Guidebook for the Beginning College Teacher.* (7th ed.) Lexington, Mass.: Heath, 1978.

Ory, J. C. *Improving Your Test Questions.* Urbana: Office of Instructional Resources, University of Illinois, 1987.

Roid, G. H. "New Technologies in the Writing of Test Items." Paper presented at the annual meeting of the American Psychological Association, Toronto, 1984. (ED 255 566)

Young, R. E. *Instructional Development Ways and Means: Testing and Grading.* Grand Forks: Office of Instructional Development, University of North Dakota, 1982. (ED 224 426)

References

Boyer, E. L. *College: The Undergraduate Experience in America.* New York: Harper & Row, 1987.

Conlan, G. *How the Essay in the College Board English Composition Test Is Scored.* Princeton, N.J.: Educational Testing Service, 1978.

Ebel, R. L. *Essentials of Educational Measurement.* (3rd ed.) Englewood Cliffs, N.J.: Prentice-Hall, 1979.

Elbow, P., and Belanoff, P. "Portfolios as a Substitute for Proficiency Examinations." *College Composition and Communication,* 1986, *37* (3), 336–339.

German, K. M. "An Applied Examination Technique for Public Speaking Classrooms." Paper presented at the annual meeting of the Speech Communication Association, Chicago, 1984. (ED 266 501)

Gronlund, N. E. *Constructing Achievement Tests.* (2nd ed.) Englewood Cliffs, N.J.: Prentice-Hall, 1977.

Guilford, J. P. *Psychometric Methods.* (2nd ed.) New York: McGraw-Hill, 1954.

Hanna, G. S., and Cashin, W. E. *Matching Instructional Objectives, Subject Matter, Tests, and Score Interpretations.* IDEA paper no. 18. Manhattan: Center for Faculty Evaluation and Development, Kansas State University, 1987.

Joint Committee of the American Education Research Association, the American Psychological Association, and the National Council on Measurement in Education. *Standards for Educational and Psychological Testing.* Washington, D.C.: American Psychological Association, 1985.

McKee, B. G., and Manning-Curtis, C. "Teacher-Constructed Classroom Tests: The Stepchild of Measurement Research." Paper presented at the annual meeting of the National Conference of Measurement in Education, New York, 1982. (ED 222 562)

Millman, J., Bishop, C. H., and Ebel, R. L. "An Analysis of Test-Wiseness." *Educational and Psychological Measurement,* 1965, *25,* 707–726.

Milton, O. *Will That Be on the Final?* Springfield, Ill.: Thomas, 1982.

Norcini, J., and Swanson, D. "Do Simulations Ever Yield Reliable Scores?" Paper presented at the annual meeting of the American Educational Research Association, New Orleans, 1988.

Reynolds, C. R., and Brown, R. T. (eds.). *Perspectives on Bias in Mental Testing.* New York: Plenum, 1984.

Scriven, M. "Objectivity and Subjectivity in Educational Research." In L. G. Thomas (ed.), *Philosophical Redirection of Education Research.* Chicago: National Society for the Study of Education, 1972.

Wigdor, A. K., and Garner, W. R. (eds.). *Ability Testing: Uses, Consequences, and Controversies.* Washington, D.C.: National Academy Press, 1982.

Jon F. Wergin is associate director of the Center for Educational Development and Faculty Resources, Virginia Commonwealth University.

*Assessment acquires meaning when it enhances the learning
of the individual student. It can do so to the degree that faculty
take responsibility for forging the components of assessment
into a process that connects expected learning outcomes with
assessment and feedback.*

Faculty as a Force to Improve Instruction Through Assessment

Georgine Loacker

Assessment can provide power for learning. It can do so if faculty set forth a process of action and map its direction so that students can steer their learning more surely. Setting forth implies taking responsibility for the what, how, and why of assessment. Mapping its direction implies connecting those parts into a process to serve the learner.

Such connections might seem obvious—what we assess should be what we teach, should be what we consider successful learning, and should be what constitutes our basis for granting academic credit and graduation. Yet more and more colleges are asking questions like "How might faculty use assessment results?" "How can we involve faculty in assessment?" Rather than a process, assessment is often a set of disconnected parts looking for a whole. Another way to put this concern is to say that our institutional mission should relate to our expected educational outcomes, which should relate to our program and course outcomes, which should relate to all aspects of our assessment process.

As faculty, we seem often to have lost the process, so that students are either completely on their own or receive occasional discrete spurts of assistance. Some theorists and practitioners of adult education say,

J. H. McMillan (ed.). *Assessing Students' Learning.*
New Directions for Teaching and Learning, no. 34. San Francisco: Jossey-Bass, Summer 1988.

"That's enough. Adults *are* self-directed learners" (Knowles, 1975; Tough, 1979; Toppins, 1987). Yet what professional dancer, swimmer, or painter has ever achieved much without a coach or mentor who somehow provided or gave direction to resources, gave information about professional expectations, and assessed the development of performance? It seems clear that people who strive to become expert learners need the same kind of attention.

In May 1987, a group of English scholars and teachers representing all the major national professional organizations in English convened at the Wayne Plantation in Maryland to project the future of their discipline and to recommend measures to secure it as meaningful and productive. They recommended a new emphasis on "classes that involve students in learning and turn instructors into coaches who learn with—rather than talk at—their students," who "focus on how students read, write, and think, rather than [on] familiarity with specific literary works." The recommendations included "study of a variety of works, including scientific papers and literary theory" and analysis of "the historical, cultural, and political dimensions of what students read," as well as "writing as an integral part of the curriculum" (Heller, 1987a, p. 9).

The Maryland conference participants recognized, as most of us do, that some of the changes described are already happening. They are happening in individual classrooms of faculty who take teaching and learning seriously. But where does assessment come in? How can faculty use assessment results? How can faculty become involved in assessment? Some of us contend that assessment—when faculty take hold of it and forge it into a process—can undergird, guard, and guide the coherence of a curriculum (Alverno College Faculty, 1985; Loacker, Cromwell, and O'Brien, 1986; Mentkowski and Loacker, 1985).

Parts of Assessment

What constitutes an assessment process that promotes student learning? The steps are predictable, yet they are difficult to accomplish: determine what is to be assessed, design the means and criteria of assessment, assess, interpret results, give feedback, and use feedback.

Determine What Is to Be Assessed. It is my experience that this deceptively simple step uncovers one's philosophy of education, as well as one's approach to the meaning of the disciplines. It uncovers what Argyris and Schön (1974) would call the espoused theory and the theory-in-use of those educators willing to articulate, analyze, and evaluate our practice. This step in the assessment process has enlivened the discussion of the professional groups that represent our disciplines (Berkhofer, 1983; Caputo, 1983; Heller, 1987a, 1987b; Rorty, 1982). What constitutes distinction or competence in the scholar or practitioner in our field? What knowledge and abilities characterize someone who is liberally educated, who specializes in English or chemistry or engineering? How does one describe knowledge in use?

Although achieving consensus about what is to be assessed is difficult, it is essential to the continuing dialogue that defines our disciplines that we articulate what we should assess and thus teach. It is especially necessary in order to make scholarly and professional expertise accessible to the learners that follow us. And whose responsibility is that articulation, if not that of the people who profess those disciplines? If we do not make that decision, we lose direction of the assessment process from the start.

Design the Means and Criteria of Assessment. Once we determine what to assess, our next task is to determine how to assess it. Again, this is a complex and stimulating undertaking. Standardized tests rarely give a sufficiently complete picture to satisfy our conception of what constitutes expertise in our fields or the refinement of understanding, insight, and judgment that characterizes a liberally educated person. Therefore, we need to set aside or at least reexamine the tests we have given for years and focus on the process that will elicit from our students the fullest possible demonstration of their ability.

If we begin by valuing the full development of student ability, we are more apt to see that an assessment process needs to include more than written performance. Portfolios, projects, simulations, exhibits, and other presentations are natural as important learning experiences. Why not ensure systematic learning by transforming them into assessments with explicit criteria and feedback? Even then, one-time testing is not enough. For a complete process of systematic learning, we also need to provide students with opportunities to relate their understandings and abilities from discipline to discipline within our institutions and to try out their competencies in integrating and applying them in external, cumulative assessments.

Assess. Checking papers may not seem the most satisfying aspect of our professional practice. However, once we elicit from students a performance of their ability, we end up with more than papers to check. We end up with samples of student behavior that require the exercise of our powers of observation and judgment to determine precisely what they reveal about a students' ability. Whether we do the assessing ourselves or train others to do it, we owe it the care that we are committed to take with any aspect of learning, for it assists us in understanding each student as a developing learner. Assessment means taking care to apply criteria and also to find any significant signs of ability that the criteria might not include. It is precisely such care that teaches students the nature of their own ability and what they might aspire to and assists in developing their own powers of self-assessment as well.

Interpret Results. The act of assessment, as just described, includes the interpretation of results, for it involves judging what a student's performance reveals about his or her ability. However, when we make inferences about a person's ability from an individual performance, we also need to relate these to the context of the specific assessment and compare them with the student's other performances of that ability. Was the performance written or oral? Was it given individually or in a group? Did the student use familiar or unfamiliar materials? What aspects and qualities of a given ability did the person show? If the task was to make verifiable inferences from historical facts, what was the extent and depth of the knowledge the person brought forth? What aspect of the context seemed to affect the response? Was the power of inference used with accuracy and originality? What modes of performance seemed to bring out what qualities?

Beneath all these questions lies the central one: what all this tells about the student's learning, its progress and its needs for future direction. The knowledge and experience that we bring to the task of interpreting assessment results for each student makes us logically responsible for it. Clearly this task demands extending faculty's advising role. Besides being disciplinary experts, we must become increasingly knowledgeable about learning and development theory, as well as about the specifics of the curriculum and students' overall academic performance. Other professionals, like counselors or evaluation specialists, might have some elements of this expertise, but they cannot be expected to have either depth of understanding in all subject areas or the day-to-day experience of each student's performance.

Give Feedback. Although individual teachers surely benefit from the kind of interpretation of results suggested here, the student is clearly the one who most needs to benefit, hence the necessity of feedback. When students try out their abilities in assessment experiences, they gradually see the experiences as natural and desirable parts of the learning process, if we design them that way and provide meaningful feedback. Such feedback contributes to the dynamic picture students should be developing of their own abilities as they take gradual control of their own learning.

Feedback can rely on one-to-one interaction or on communication with an entire class or small groups within a class. It can be a well-worded sentence or a spoken comment. Whatever the form, we have found in our research at Alverno that feedback is meaningful if at a teachable moment it motivates further development (Mentkowski and Doherty, 1984). It is meaningful if it informs and enhances a student's power of self-assessment.

Use Feedback. No matter how meaningful feedback may be, it loses its meaning if no one uses it. It has been our experience at Alverno that the more connected feedback is to the abilities students are working to develop, to the criteria they are striving to meet, and to other performances they have provided, the more apt they are to use it for understanding and further development of their knowledge and abilities.

The teacher's use of feedback needs to connect to the broader picture he or she has of each student's development, if changes in teaching strategies are to affect the learning of the individual students. At Alverno, faculty have reported that such feedback contributes significantly to their own development, serving as an index to the quality and clarity of their teaching and signaling the need to review how certain ideas were presented.

Who Benefits

If learning is enhanced by the way faculty design assessment as a system, learners also benefit. Just as certainly, instructors benefit to the degree that they have committed themselves to the development of the learner. The learner's success is their success.

More directly, however, faculty who have approached assessment, as described here, find that it improves their instruction immediately and concretely in several ways:

- Provides a means of clarifying what we should be teaching
- Assists in refining expectations of the level and quality of student performance
- Provides a means of actively involving the student in the learning process
- Requires adapting pedagogy to the needs of student learning
- Provides feedback on how well instructional strategies are working for each student
- Brings about collaboration of faculty.

Assessment provides a means of clarifying what we should be teaching: what the disciplines mean and might come to mean. If we agree to design assessment as it is described here, we are agreeing to be explicit in identifying what we will assess. When that is within our control, we will be more apt to teach it. We will also begin to have a sharper sense of contributing to the future shape of our disciplines. I am not talking about creating endless lists of behavioral objectives. Rather, I am calling for a start in saying to students that expertise in biology means some specific abilities, like being able to interpret, use, or design models that illustrate biological mechanisms or constructs in specialized areas in biology. Again, expertise in psychology may mean abilities like analyzing behavior within multiple theoretical frameworks supported by empirical data. Once we say that to students, we are on the way to holding them to the development of this expertise by assessing and crediting them for it. Not everyone might agree with the statements of abilities we make, but in starting discussion we keep clarifying our own position, and students will feel "in on" the understanding of their future fields and perhaps develop more trust in their teachers as the current experts in these fields.

One assistant professor of communication has explained the quality of interaction that explicitness of outcomes encourages: "I spent a number of years feeling frustrated by my inability to incorporate my care for each individual student into my evaluation of them within the traditional structure of a freshman-level curriculum. Assessment has brought me from the uncomfortable position—where I knew intuitively what I expected from my students, but was unable to express it—to the point where I can now state my expectations clearly enough for both the students and me to understand. And that clarity in turn has enabled me to 'sit down beside' my students—to help them individually begin to develop a process of self-understanding" (Judith Bergan, personal communication).

A professor of political science suggests the broader institutional effects of making outcomes explicit: "Assessment has helped us refine the notion of academic planning. Not only do we have a better idea of where we are, but we are better able to clarify and operationally conceptualize where we want to be. In turn, these benefits serve to generate a sense of dynamism among faculty and staff, which facilitates the creative leaps required to narrow the gaps between the *is* and the *ought*" (Stuart Vorkink, personal communication).

Assessment assists in refining expectations of the level and quality of college performance. This happens when faculty identify criteria, interpret results, and use feedback. Once we state criteria and note what our students are able to produce in the best of circumstances, it is easier to see when students are not going beyond what they were already able to demonstrate in secondary school. It is also easier to see when we are demanding graduate-quality work of all our students, instead of encouraging it in those who are ready to reach it. Best of all, we begin to have a more precise understanding of the unique facets of an ability expressing itself in various individuals.

When confronted with our own criteria and samples of how our students meet them, we are more apt to make even the simple admission that very few students can be expected to write, in thirty or even sixty minutes, a well-structured essay with brilliant insights and well-documented inferences, graced by compelling style. We are also more apt to find ways to make our requirements work for the student. An assistant professor of professional communication puts it this way: "Especially in teaching and learning through written communication, assessment has assisted us to move from an amorphous 'there's something wrong here' to a specific area to focus on for development. What is more, it has called to our attention 'what is right here' and working. In essence, assessment has aided the teaching-learning process for me by providing a means for increased precision and compassion" (Joyce Fey, personal communication).

Assessment provides a means of actively involving the student in his or her own learning process and that of other students. At Alverno, we find that students begin to take hold of their own learning process when we set forth what abilities they are required to develop and what standards they must meet. Knowledge of expectations and criteria gives them a point of entry. A professor of English confirms this when he says, "The criteria we use to evaluate student performance in writing are also used by students to assess their own work. This process of self-assessment makes possible thorough revision of papers and increases a student's understanding of the composing process" (Larry Corse, personal communication). Using the criteria with some success encourages students to proceed, especially when feedback from faculty confirms their judgments. As one fourth-year Alverno student described it in a presentation to other students:

> I began to view myself not as just a good student or bad student but more as an individual, and I started to take responsibility for my work. Something happened every time I had to write down how I thought I did on certain criteria. By having to say concretely, "Yes, I did do well in setting context, and I think I was weak in drawing a meaningful conclusion," I had to own my work. When you give yourself a low rating, then you are going to have to justify it. You'll say, "Why did I do this? Why didn't I work harder at it? Where did I go wrong? I am going to try to improve upon this."
>
> Then I began to take credit for what I did well and what I needed to improve on. Once I did serious self-assessing, I couldn't pass the blame on and say, "Well, the instructor didn't like me." It also helped to hear from a variety of different instructors that I met specific criteria.
>
> Then take creativity. I think it helped to free me up when I could say, "OK, I know I'm meeting the basic criteria. Now I can try some creative things. Maybe I will make a total fool of myself as far as trying something new."

The kinds of assessment that have assisted this student in involving herself in her learning have consistently required her to use her knowledge to analyze constructs or situations, to make refined judgments and decisions, and to draw conclusions supported by clear evidence. In a regular art assessment for each semester, for example, she may have been required to select and present works she has produced during that semester and accompany their presentation with an oral explanation and evaluation before representative art faculty. In a biology assessment, the student may have participated as a member of a team of experts on a public health agency task force assigned to study specified alarming shifts in fertility rates and birth defects in a given metropolitan area. From the perspective of a given area of expertise, like microbiology or genetics, she would have set forth to her colleagues her process of analysis, including initial questions, assumptions, determination of hypothesis and testing procedures, selection of methodologies, and the relation of her approach of inquiry to that of the other experts on the team (Loacker and others, 1984).

Such assessments enable students to experience learning as a process. When they become more aware of what they can accomplish in their education and what successful demonstration of ability looks like, they become not only better at assessing their own performances but also more willing and able to assess their peers and to collaborate in their learning. They also begin to see the value of assessment by their peers and feedback from them.

A good example of how students can develop their ability to assess their own performances and those of their peers in a systematically refined way is the performance assessment labs initiated by the music faculty at Alverno. These labs are group extensions of the students' private lessons. Those studying in the same applied music area meet once a week in groups of not more than fifteen to hear and respond to each other's performances. Each student is videotaped for a cumulative record of his or her performances. Through the use of explicit criteria, students learn how multiple elements contribute to the effectiveness of a total performance. They also learn how to use appropriate technical language to describe subtle differences in style and to bring together frameworks from music theory and history and combine them with their own experiences of performance and interpretation to make more sophisticated judgments.

Assessment requires adapting pedagogy to the needs of student learning. When faculty identify what is to be assessed and require that students demonstrate it on the basis of criteria, they begin to see that students need more than faculty input of information or concepts. They realize that students need time to practice analyzing data (whether historical or scientific), drawing conclusions from data, and making judgments regarding meaning and relevance. They need time to practice articulating what they have learned in individual oral presentations and in group problem-solving situations, as well as in writing. They need feedback on the quality and effects of their practice. Assessment makes those needs more apparent to faculty, so that reexamining one's pedagogical theory and approach and adapting it to those needs becomes inevitable for those who create an assessment process and attend to its implications.

We have much to learn from developments in the research and pedagogy of written composition over the past thirty years. Writing becomes learning for students when we give them time, space, and careful assistance with the long process of composing, instead of just looking at their products and teaching them conventions of appropriate style. Writing becomes an expression of their own understanding of disciplinary concepts when they make it a vehicle for thinking through those concepts, as well as a statement of already formed conclusions and positions. The principles of writing across the curriculum could profitably translate into principles for learning across the curriculum.

Speaking can also be utilized to effectively assess students. If we think of our students as future presenters at our professional meetings and conferences, we can easily imagine what needs to be done. How will they learn to think through their disciplines, articulate existing and new concepts, and become at ease in talking about them to colleagues unless they have practice, assessment and feedback? They need models, besides ourselves, at all stages of the profession. In addition to speech assessment within disciplines, another helpful strategy devised at Alverno is to replace the introductory speech textbook with a set of videos that illustrate all aspects of effective speaking through student samples taken from recorded assessment performances.

Focusing on assessment of ability directs faculty toward a new way of viewing not only textbooks but also every other aspect of the teaching-learning situation. Faculty from various institutions and fields have found individual ways of describing that view: "I write better, more productive assignments, and students write better papers now that both they and I know ahead of time what the writing assessment criteria are"; "I found very quickly that my students perceived science as all content. Nor did they have any understanding that the so-called scientific method might be applicable to other disciplines. So I've switched my thinking and my teaching. I try to help students see that the scientific method is an extension of their critical thinking experience. I realize that since science is a process, they have to *do* it. I now have them do much more in class"; "Rather than concentrating solely upon factual content, my bias is toward teaching a conceptual framework upon which facts may be organized and analyzed. Therefore I attempted to provide testing material to examine the ability to handle information as well as to recall it. Ideally, assessment will allow me to adjust my balance between these two aspects of teaching"; "Thinking of assessment as learning has encouraged me to view every experience in a course as potentially instructive. Testing as a way to find out what the student knows is replaced by the notion of assessment as an opportunity to help students learn more about their abilities and how to keep improving. This means that I design assessment experiences with as much concern for what students can learn about themselves as for what I can learn about them" (William Pasch, Robert Paoletti, Gerald Vaughn, Timothy Riordan, personal communication).

When faculty begin to view their teaching from the student's perspective, change becomes a self-chosen strategy, rather than the resisted threat it can sometimes be. The view extends beyond a specific teaching-learning situation to the large questions of the profession and professional development.

Assessment provides feedback on how well instructional strategies are working for each student and on the quality and unique characteristics of each student's abilities. Because the kind of assessment described here is designed as a process, one can assume some relationship between student performance and instructional strategies. Just as ongoing feedback tells a student how well he or she is doing, it tells a teacher how much and what kinds of assistance students need.

"Especially through self-assessment, I find out how secure students are about their ability and about their knowledge," explains a professor of English at Alverno. "I find out whether they feel in control of their learning; I discover, indeed, whether they are really learning or simply able to complete an assignment (sometimes by blind luck). For example, one of my first-semester students was analyzing assumptions in a speech she had listened to. Her answers were appropriate, but in her self-assessment she indicated having difficulty in determining assumptions. She said that she did not feel she really understood what assumptions are or how to go about stating them. This was a case in which the student had somehow given the 'right' answer but clearly did not have control over the ability required of her. Without the self-assessment I might not have realized what this student needed."

Assessment of this kind looks at results in relation to criteria, rather than results in quantified form; therefore, differences in student performance become more meaningful. They distinguish specific aspects of an ability. One student consistently makes credible intuitive judgments about a literary character, for example, before having sufficient evidence to support them. Another carefully accumulates accurate observations and draws out patterns before forming judgments.

Assessments also show differences in qualitative characteristics that change the nature of a student's expression of ability. Where one student shows logical clarity of thought, another shows imaginative clarity of thought. Where one student shows independence of thought, another shows awareness of his or her own thinking processes.

Assessment brings about collaboration of faculty for the sake of the student. Once we are explicit about what is to be assessed, articulate criteria for it, assess for it, and keep students aware of precisely how well they are doing, we necessarily begin a dialogue with our colleagues. We find ways of agreeing on how to assist students to build on what they have already developed. If we agree to have any external assessment at all, only consensus at some level can make it possible. The process is worth the struggle, for it forces us all to reset our sights and assist students in becoming scholars and practitioners.

This does not seem to happen unless assessment goes beyond a single course and to programs or departments. At Alverno, because assessment is designed to work throughout the entire curriculum, faculty collaboration has become a dramatic outcome of the assessment process. Collaboration in turn has become a growing cause of effectiveness.

At two very different kinds of institutions, colleagues have found that faculty-directed assessment results in collaboration that has productive effects. A professor of philosophy at one school affirms that working to understand and use assessment has significantly refined his views on teaching-learning strategies, and he attributes the relative ease with which he has been able to implement those views to the climate of collaboration: "I believe that teaching disciplinary content, though necessary, does not suffice for the development within students of those dispositions, attitudes, and skills that characterize a mature learner. It's difficult to involve students Socratically in the learning process, but through the increased faculty collaboration and support here . . . , the task has become easier" (Henry Nardone, personal communication).

An associate professor of art history at another institution says that when she met with her department members to design an assessment for majors, she "found it exciting—as did even those who were initially reluctant to get involved—to think as a group in a new way. We had to clarify to each other what we teach," she said, "and discuss in a focused way what skills we expect of our students, in addition to knowledge. I am determined to devise a strategy to build in such ongoing discussion" (Dorothy Habel, personal communication).

External Rewards

Accustomed as faculty are to making some aspects of teaching their own reward, respect for teaching will be unrecognized until we see it take concrete form within educational policy. Assessment shares the same lot, but there are places to begin. One such place is in criteria for promotion. If faculty know that expert teaching defines their status as surely as, if not more surely than, published research, they will seek ways to improve their teaching and will find assessment a powerful vehicle for improvement.

Assessment, as described here, encourages explicitness of criteria to describe successful performance. This enables assessors and students to reach agreement in their judgments. As faculty experience that with their students, it is inevitable that they will apply the principles to their own performance. They will see the importance of having explicit criteria for promotion. Once criteria for promotion become explicit, any omission of effective teaching among the criteria becomes more glaring.

Another encouragement for assessment is the awarding of fellowships for summer work. We may argue that assessment design is part of one's teaching responsibility, but faculty are not always apt to see it that way until they begin to design and implement the process. Therefore, it seems important to fund creative starts. Even after faculty see the value of assessment, they need to feel the force of an institutional commitment behind them, and institutions need to find ways to make their commitment apparent.

Most postsecondary faculty feel rewarded for their published research, yet it is not always clear how that research improves their teaching. If institutions would make it clear that they strongly encourage research on teaching—in fact, require it—they would make room for research that could improve teaching by improving assessment. If postsecondary educational institutions want faculty to take assessment seriously, it seems imperative that they find ways to show faculty that they take their teaching seriously, their research on teaching seriously, and consequently their assessment seriously.

Assessment as Its Own Reward

It has been our experience at Alverno that when faculty take charge of assessment as part of the learning process, assessment enhances teaching and in fact newly excites faculty about teaching. Most faculty in postsecondary education readily admit that they were not trained to teach. Beyond knowledge of our discipline, enthusiasm for it, and some communications skills, we have had little to say about what constitutes effective teaching. Assessment of student performance gives us insights into what effective teaching might mean, because it makes learning more visible. Also, as students become more aware of their own performance— what it means in terms of criteria, what it includes, what it lacks, and how it changes—they become more aware of how they learn, and they share this awareness with faculty. Alverno faculty find that these comments by students, made in regular self-assessment exercises, are fairly typical. A first-semester student who has not yet declared a major said, "I saw that the essay in which I tried to write about my science class was very poor because I don't really understand electromagnetic waves, atoms, and balancing equations. My writing was confusing because I was confused. I need to discuss these concepts with someone, because I find that I can't just get them by reading about them. When I wrote about humanities I did a better job. There I had already learned that I can no longer get away with mere memorization and that I need to apply what I learn in order to understand it." A fifth-semester business and management major wrote, "Leadership skills is one area that I want to concentrate on. In my last small-group encounter, the theory I came closest to was path-goal theory. I gave directive leadership in stating our goal, was very supportive of others' ideas by encouraging them in their ideas, used achievement-oriented leadership in trying to accomplish our goal, and used participative skills in our jointly reaching our goal. This confirms for me that my leadership skills come across best in a teamwork environment. What I need to concentrate on in my advanced-level work is developing leadership skills when I am placed in a decision-making situation. I have not had much experience in this type of leading, so I need practice in situations that require individual decisions."

For faculty who see teaching as their profession and take pride in its practice, these observations provide affirmation and excitement. Gradually, faculty see that sound assessment, in their hands, can provide a powerful means of demonstrating effective teaching. Such a prospect is very far from the idea of using students' test scores to measure teachers' effectiveness. Such a prospect can help transform our profession.

References

Alverno College Faculty. *Assessment at Alverno College.* Milwaukee, Wisc.: Alverno Productions, 1985.

Argyris, C., and Schön, D. *Theory in Practice: Increasing Professional Effectiveness.* San Francisco: Jossey-Bass, 1974.

Berkhofer, R. F. "The Two New Histories: Competing Paradigms for Interpreting the American Past." *OAH Newsletter*, 1983, *2* (2), 9–12.

Caputo, J. D. "The Thought of Being and the Conversation of Mankind: The Case of Heidegger and Rorty." *The Review of Metaphysics*, 1983, *36* (3), 661–685.

Heller, S. "English Teachers Favor Emphasis on How to Read, Write, Think, Rather Than on Becoming Familiar with Specific Literary Works." *Chronicle of Higher Education*, August 5, 1987a, pp. 9–10.

Heller, S. "Literature Scholars Struggle to Find New Ways to Instruct the English Professors of Tomorrow." *Chronical of Higher Education*, April 15, 1987b, pp. 15–17.

Knowles, M. S. *Self-Directed Learning: A Guide for Learners and Teachers.* New York: Association Press, 1975.

Loacker, G., Cromwell, L., Fey, J., and Rutherford, D. *Analysis and Communication at Alverno: An Approach to Critical Thinking.* Milwaukee, Wisc.: Alverno Productions, 1984.

Loacker, G., Cromwell, L., and O'Brien, K. "Assessment in Higher Education: To Serve the Learner." In C. Adelman (ed.), *Assessment in American Higher Education.* Washington, D.C.: U.S. Department of Education, 1986.

Mentkowski, M., and Doherty, A. *Careering after College: Establishing the Validity of Abilities for Later Careering and Professional Performance.* Final report to the National Institute of Education: Overview and Summary. Milwaukee, Wisc.: Alverno Productions, 1984.

Mentkowski, M., and Loacker, G. "Assessing and Validating the Outcomes of

32

College." In P. Ewell (ed.), *Assessing Education Outcomes*. New Directions for Institutional Research. no. 47. San Francisco: Jossey-Bass, 1985.

Rorty, R. M. "Hermeneutics, General Studies and Teaching Synergos." *Selected Papers from the Synergos Seminars*. Vol. 2. Fairfax, Va.: George Mason University, 1982.

Toppins, A. D. "Teaching Students to Teach Themselves." *College Teaching*, 1987, *35* (3), 95–99.

Tough, A. *The Adult's Learning Project*. Toronto: Ontario Institute for Studies in Education, 1979.

Georgine Loacker is professor of English and chair of the Assessment Council at Alverno College. She is a coauthor of Assessment at Alverno College *(1985) and has written numerous articles on educational assessment.*

The assessment of critical thinking can be greatly improved as faculty identify needs, goals, and a conception of critical thinking and integrate this information with known assessment strategies.

Assessing Critical Thinking Across the Curriculum

C. Blaine Carpenter, James C. Doig

What professor would deny the importance of enhancing students' critical thinking? Recent national reports and publications identify critical thinking as an essential ingredient of higher education. However, while skill in critical thinking is a needed outcome, there has been relatively little discussion of how to test and evaluate a student's capability to think critically. In this chapter we will review assessment procedures that can be used in the classroom and on the institutional level to measure critical thinking. Our emphasis is on techniques that can be used across the curriculum.

Defining the Skill

The first issue of assessment is knowing what will be measured. It is important, then, to begin with an appropriate conception of critical thinking. There are many choices here, and selecting an appropriate one should not be arbitrary. A definition of critical thinking should be clear and sufficiently detailed to guide the assessment process. While we do not discuss the various conceptions, we urge that the assessment process begin with a consideration of possible conceptions. There are good sources to consider (Beyer, 1987; Ennis, 1987; McPeck, 1981; Meyers, 1986;

J. H. McMillan (ed.). *Assessing Students' Learning.*
New Directions for Teaching and Learning, no. 34. San Francisco: Jossey-Bass, Summer 1988.

Sternberg, 1985; and Young, 1980). Ennis (1987) for example, defines critical thinking broadly, including many different skills. Examples of such skills include judging the credibility of a source, deduction, induction, identifying stated and unstated assumptions, and identifying fallacy labels like *name calling, straw person,* and *non sequitur.* The process of agreeing on a conception of critical thinking can be time consuming, especially if a common definition is used in different disciplines. The quality of the assessment, though, depends on this important step.

Choosing an Approach to Assess Critical Thinking

There are several points to keep in mind in selecting or developing an approach to assess critical thinking. First, it should clearly describe the processes, skills, or strategies to be assessed. Such descriptions should be complete enough to give a detailed idea of the nature of each aspect of critical thinking to be assessed, the procedures to be followed in the assessment, and criteria to judge evidence of critical thinking. A successful approach will state how the thinking processes, skills, or strategies work together and will identify the form or type of thinking that is to be assessed. Approaches also should be selected or developed with regard to student motivation and the environments in which students live (Sternberg, 1984). For instance, the ethnic, religious, or cultural values and outlooks of students may require that instruction and exercises in a critical thinking program be designed to develop students' awareness of their environments. Finally, the faculty should clarify its assumptions relative to the prerequisite knowledge and skills that students need prior to engaging in college-level critical thinking.

Generally speaking, approaches to the assessment of critical thinking will rely either on standardized examinations or on locally developed, performance-based instruments. Descriptions and critiques of a number of approaches to assessing critical thinking are found in Segal, Chipman, and Glaser (1985). A discussion of developing complete verbal descriptions of processes, skills, and strategies can be found in Beyer (1987). Meyers (1986) suggests that visual models are often more helpful than verbal descriptions. Visual models taking the form of diagrams can range from one that concretely represents a tree, composed of circles coinciding with concepts used in thinking operations, to one that abstractly represents the steps in problem solving.

To summarize, an informed choice of an approach to assessing critical thinking can be made only after faculty have reached the explicit determinations mentioned above; that is, by asking and answering these questions: What do we think critical thinking is? How do the critical thinking skills, processes, and strategies work together, and what aspects or combinations of them do we wish to assess? What are our students like? What are their motivations, and what are their environments? What are our assumptions relative to the knowledge and abilities that students need prior to engaging in college-level critical thinking?

Standardized Examinations. There are several standardized tests that may be appropriate for assessing critical thinking skills. These exams are not specifically geared to the distinctiveness of institutional programs, and because they measure general conceptions of critical thinking, they will not assess more specific, institutionally defined skills of individual students. These tests have good reliability; national norms are usually also available. Both Ennis (1985a, 1985b) and Beyer (1987) summarize existing standardized tests of critical thinking. Following are brief descriptions of some of these tests.

Cornell Critical Thinking Test, Level 2. This test was developed by Robert H. Ennis and Jason Millman and is available from Midwest Publications (P.O. Box 448, Pacific Grove, CA 93950). It contains 52 items for advanced or gifted high school students, college students, and other adults. There are also sections on induction, deduction, observation, credibility, defining, and assumption identification.

New Jersey Test of Reasoning Skills. This test was developed by Virginia Shipman and is available from IAPC, Test Division (Montclair State College, Upper Montclair, NJ 07043). The exam includes 50 items, untimed, for grades four through college. It contains items testing syllogistic reasoning, contradictions, causal relationships, assumption identification, induction, good reasons, and other topics.

Watson-Glaser Critical Thinking Appraisal (Forms A and B). This test was developed by Goodwin Watson and Edward Glaser and is available from the Psychological Corporation (c/o Harcourt Brace Jovanovich, 7500 Old Oak Blvd., Cleveland, OH 44130). It contains 80 items on two forms, timed or untimed, for grades nine through adult, as well as sections on inference, assumption identification, deduction, conclusion logically following beyond a reasonable doubt (interpretation), and argument evaluation.

Ennis-Weir Critical Thinking Essay Test. This test was developed by Robert H. Ennis and Eric Weir. Like the Cornell test, this is published by Midwest Publications. It is aimed at grades seven through college. Students are given forty minutes in which to write a letter in response to a "letter to the editor" that posits a particular position. Students critique the thinking exhibited in the letter. The test measures getting to the point, seeing reasons and assumptions, stating one's point, offering some good reasons, seeing other possibilities, and responding appropriately (for example, avoiding irrelevance, circularity, and overgeneralization).

The Academic Profile. This instrument comes from the Educational Testing Service (College and University Programs, Princeton, NJ 08541-0001). In 1987 ETS piloted a new assessment service for general education. The Academic Profile is intended to measure four academic skills (college-level reading, college-level writing, critical thinking, and using mathematical data) in three major discipline groups (humanities, social sciences, and natural sciences). The profile is available in long or short forms and reports a separate score for each skill and discipline group, with a total score. Thus, The Academic Profile provides a general assessment of critical thinking.

Locally Developed Instruments. For faculty whose goals require them to develop their own performance-based instruments, two types of assessment of critical thinking outcomes are most common: (1) paper-and-pencil items specifically intended to test skills, processes, or strategies, and (2) observation of student behavior. The former is used in regularly assigned classroom tests and is recommended for assessment of critical thinking as part of a course or program. However, regarding paper-and-pencil tests, a distinction should be made between assessment of newly introduced thinking skills or processes and those previously taught and assessed. In the case of newly introduced skills, all items designed for assessment are best grouped in a special section of the test. Further, to adequately assess such a skill, it is not enough to ask students to use the skill; they should also be required to define it, identify an example of its use, use it several times, and explain how to use it. An advantage of this approach is that different levels of proficiency can be assessed. The first level is attained by students who are able to define the skill correctly and identify an example of its use. The second level is reached by students who use the skill successfully, and the third level involves the ability to explain the skill. When a skill previously taught and assessed is being reassessed, the initial level of proficiency can be assumed (Beyer, 1987).

Since thinking skills are seldom used in isolation, one should be prepared to assess more complex thinking operations performed by students. Items similar to those on the SAT are a possibility. A situation students are to think about can be presented in a short paragraph, followed by a series of multiple-choice questions, each requiring the student to employ a different thinking skill (Beyer, 1987). Items in standardized examinations can serve as examples for locally developed tests of critical thinking.

Essay tests also can be developed by faculty. The criteria used to evaluate answers should be stated explicitly before students attempt an exam and should be focused on the thinking skills being assessed, not on the knowledge or writing skills demonstrated. Various types of essay questions can be developed. For example, data can be presented in different ways (written, orally, audiovisually), and students can respond to questions in a specified number of paragraphs. The answers can be graded for one or a combination of skills. Students can be asked to explain the use of some selected aspect or aspects of thinking, and the audience can range from an instructor to a less well informed student. Students can also be given essay assignments on regular subject-matter topics and asked to attach to their completed essays brief explanations of the thinking processes involved in their writing (Beyer, 1987).

Meyers (1986) details the characteristics of writing assignments that are effective for teaching critical thinking. Two of these characteristics also appear to be useful in designing assessment instruments. First, essay assignments should follow a stepwise development of critical thinking skills. Since students learn by practicing the component abilities of critical thinking, assignments should begin by requiring the use of simple cognitive skills (observing or organizing) and then move gradually in subsequent assignments to more complex skills, such as synthesizing and evaluating. A second characteristic of effective writing assignments is their relation to real problems or issues and students' experiences. For example, instead of asking students to write on the United States constitutional guarantee of free speech, the assignment might be: "Your roommate is organizing a campus protest against his or her government professor, who is teaching the theories of Karl Marx. What can you say to your roommate in terms of the constitutional guarantee of free speech, as it relates to his or her protest?" A more accurate picture of students' abilities will result when students are asked to struggle with problems that they actually encounter. In addition to discussions of the above characteristics, Meyers presents helpful descriptions of five types of writing assignments for critical thinking, two examples being brief summaries and problem-solving exercises.

An additional paper-and-pencil method of assessment involves determining certain general forms or types of critical thinking (for example, problem solving and decision making) that employ a variety of skills or strategies in an integrated fashion. Since it is the general form of thinking that is to be assessed, and not the individual skills (which can vary with the context), this is accomplished with performance criteria specific to the general form of thinking.

Besides the paper-and-pencil methods, assessment can be achieved through observation of student behavior. Here, the emphasis is on what students do as they go about developing answers. Costa (1984) has listed observable behaviors that indicate effective thinking. These include persisting in a thinking task and applying alternative methods until a goal is reached; deliberately planning how to execute a thinking task by clarifying goals, identifying givens, and carefully selecting methods and data; giving and requesting evidence and reasoning in support of assertions; and using and insisting on precise language. Beyer (1987) offers examples of forms for reporting observations.

Another possible approach for observing student behavior is based on the paired problem-solving techniques described by Whimbey (1977).

Students work in pairs on thinking tasks, and while one student does the actual work of thinking and reports aloud what he or she is thinking, the other student keeps track of the process to ensure that no steps are skipped and no rules violated. A handbook by Whimbey and Lochhead (1982) incorporates this approach. Paired problem solving is utilized in the Integrated Science Laboratory at Alverno College (Loacker and others, 1984).

Some Institutional Examples

A number of institutions have made great strides recently in assessing critical thinking. In this section we describe six of them.

Northeast Missouri State University. This institution attempts to assess critical thinking as one aspect of the "intellectual value added" by classroom instruction. The key components of the assessment are nationally standardized tests administered to all students near the close of the liberal arts portion of their studies, and exams given during the semester prior to graduation. The tests given near the end of the student's liberal arts studies can be of two types. Since nearly all students have taken ACT tests prior to enrollment, half of each sophomore class is given an ACT retest to determine individual and cohort learning growth in four areas: English, mathematics, social science, and natural science. The other half of any sophomore class will have taken the ACT-COMP during the second semester of the freshman year and is retested with ACT-COMP toward the end of the sophomore year to determine individual and cohort learning growth in six liberal learning skill areas, one of which, problem solving, is related to critical thinking. Also, many of the items in the ACT-COMP require the use of thinking skills that some believe are a part of critical thinking (analysis, application, and synthesis) (Smith, 1986, pp. 290–291).

University of Tennessee. This institution also administers the ACT-COMP, in this case to freshmen and seniors, to assess learning growth in the six areas, including problem solving. The ACT-COMP data on students' skills in solving problems, communicating, and clarifying values, in conjunction with performance on comprehensive exams in major fields, have led faculty to make changes in structure of courses, number of written assignments, and opportunities for students to apply their knowledge and skills through problem solving, term projects, field trips, and internships. Test results and faculty discussion of them have led to the development of more specific objectives for student learning and a better relation of course content to objectives (Banta and Fisher, 1986).

Alverno College. Critical thinking for Alverno is closely linked to the skill of analysis, although it also includes evaluating ideas, identifying problems, considering values, and finding creative approaches to problems. Analysis is also seen as varying with different kinds of knowledge. Hence, Alverno focuses attention on developing critical thinking skills within particular knowledge contexts (for example, the skills of the scientific method and literary analysis). Alverno and the other institutions yet to be described focus assessment on student learning in relation to precisely stated outcomes developed both for courses within programs and for programs as a whole. Further, assessment occurs within each course and becomes a means of determining how well each student is developing a critical thinking outcome. This type of assessment involves eliciting several samples of a student's critical thinking, judging those samples by publicly stated criteria, and providing feedback to the student about his or her performance.

Analysis is defined as the ability to examine the parts of a whole in order to gain better understanding of the parts and the whole. In each discipline, students learn about and analyze something unique to that discipline. An integrative approach has been developed that emphasizes the systematic "breaking open" of the ability, a sequential learning process that involves observing, inferring, making relationships, and integrating within a disciplinary context. Also emphasized is the translating of the "generic" ability into the concrete and specific terms of individual disciplines. Recognition of how different disciplines involve analysis is found by translating the basic analytical sequence into the language of each discipline. For example, one asks what it means to analyze, observe, infer, make relationships, and integrate the knowledge base in biology, history, literature, philosophy, and so on. These analytical abilities are also tied to the student's communication competence.

Alverno's assessment of an ability is initially broken into levels, ranging from what students should be able to do when entering college to what is expected of them by the time they graduate. In the case of analysis and the connected ability of communication, six levels are distinguished, with the first four general and required of all students and the last two specialized and appropriate to the student's major. These six levels are observing accurately, making justifiable inferences, relating parts or elements in patterns, integrating patterns into coherent systems, comparing and testing frameworks in a discipline, and integrating frameworks into a professional synthesis.

These levels identify standards by which student performance can be assessed and offer expectations for student development. The levels are not viewed as a rigid sequence of steps, but simply as a logical approach to assessing (and teaching) the analytical process.

Alverno College breaks each level into a more specific set of criteria. These criteria are developed with the various discipline faculties and then synthesized into generic criteria. For example, at level 4 ("Integrates patterns into coherent systems") they are described in this way:

- Out of an explicit framework, articulates and distinguishes between observations, inferences, and relationships in work under investigation
- Shows awareness of assumptions, implications, and limitations of any framework used
- Identifies principle(s) that organize(s) or account(s) for ways that elements relate in the work
- Articulates how above principle(s) provide(s) meaning in the work under investigation
- Shows awareness of how the affective and intuitive relate to the cognitive in one's own analyzing process and abilities.

The final element identified for each discipline and course is the performance that the student is expected to undertake; that is, an assignment is geared to a specific disciplinary task on a determined level, which includes specification of audience, purpose, and other circumstances aiding the student to write coherently about a given situation (Loacker and others, 1984).

Alverno College, through its emphasis across the curriculum on the generic ability of analysis, with assessment occurring on several levels, focuses the student's attention on one cognitive process at a time. For example, Alverno's level 4 appears similar to what others call synthesis (Bloom, 1956; Beyer, 1987). By implication, then, analysis or critical thinking appears as the integration of a variety of cognitive skills.

King's College. At King's College, all students are required to take a critical thinking course. In this course, students are expected to develop and defend reasonable beliefs, to assess the beliefs of others, and to develop rational self-awareness (Hammerbacher, 1987). Initial instruction in this course is focused on aspects of thinking (for example, argumentation and rhetorical use of language), and subsequent assessment is focused on the use of these various aspects in a variety of knowledge contexts across the curriculum. Assessment measures for the critical thinking course are well defined: a pretest to assess entry-level competence; three tests of the student's knowledge of the content and processes appropriate to the course competencies; frequent quizzes and textbook exercises; two major writing assignments, one a critical analysis and evaluation of an extended argument, and the other an argumentative essay on a controversial topic; and a posttest (usually the same as the pretest).

Unlike Alverno, King's College has not specified criteria for a variety of levels of competence in the use of critical thinking. Instead, a list of criteria has been developed, from which faculty select items appropriate to the particular degree of complexity of critical thinking to be assessed. Accordingly, the student:

- Demonstrates recall and understanding of the pivotal concepts of inductive and deductive reasoning

- Identifies an argument and distinguishes support from conclusion
- Identifies such problems as ambiguity, vagueness, and emotionally loaded language
- Identifies crucial fallacies in arguments
- Summarizes and reconstructs an argument contained in an extended prose passage
- Draws appropriate inferences from given data
- Recognizes the hidden assumptions and the implied premises and conclusions of an argument
- Distinguishes subarguments from the main argument in a prose passage
- Separates a problem into discrete units and sets forth evidence in separate, meaningful categories
- Uses the results of appropriate research (library, expert opinion, survey, poll, experiment) in the analysis, construction, and evaluation of arguments
- Identifies and explains the reasoning process applied to various disciplines and demonstrates that process by constructing a strong argument in one of those fields, preferably his or her own major
- Recognizes and performs the basic functions of deductive and inductive reasoning
- Chooses and defends an appropriate course of action from among a number of possible alternatives
- Relates an argument to broader issues and concerns
- Evaluates the acceptability of premises, their relevance to a conclusion, and the adequacy of their support of that conclusion.

The use of skills inherent in such cognitive processes as observing, clarifying, and evaluating is implicitly and, in some cases, explicitly expected of the students as they complete their assigned tasks. Thus, despite differences in terminology and procedure, it appears that both King's College and Alverno use assessment to develop similar abilities in their students.

Clayton State College. Like King's College, Clayton State has chosen to develop a course focused on teaching students the basics of critical thinking. This initial course focuses on instruction in the cognitive process skills—for example, observing, analyzing, and evaluating—and on students' use of combinations of these skills in a variety of knowledge contexts.

Assessment at Clayton State College is similar to that at Alverno College and King's College. Several samples of a student's critical thinking are judged according to publicly stated criteria, and feedback is provided to students. With this form of assessment as its goal, the college has defined critical thinking as information or knowledge gathering and reasoning characterized by careful and continual thought. The college also envisions the process of critical thinking in terms of a continuum. One extreme is characterized by a contemplative approach, and the other by a highly structured approach. Although thinking may occur at any point along this imaginary "thinking continuum," the program involves the assessment of student performance at only two points. One point, thinking characterized by a highly structured and formulaic approach, is termed *problem solving decision making,* where the emphasis is on a product (that is, a solution or a decision). At the other extreme of the continuum is inquiry, a more contemplative, less structured approach that results in an informed judgment. In any particular exercise of critical thinking, the student uses a combination of the cognitive process skills. The combination is determined by the purpose of the exercise, the material or subject matter of the exercise, and the appropriate form or type of critical thinking. Thus, Clayton State's assessments are different from those of Alverno and King's College in that emphasis is placed on assessment of the use of the cognitive process skills in two different types of applications, inquiry and problem solving/decision making.

For each of these two forms of critical thinking, criteria have been developed, and each form has four performance ratings. This arrangement enables an assessor to provide feedback to students on their levels of abilities. Clayton's criterion 1 for problem solving/decision making is shown in Exhibit 1; criterion 2 for inquiry is shown in Exhibit 2 (Clayton State College, 1985).

Exhibit 1. Criterion 1, Problem Solving/Decision Making, Clayton State College

Problem Identification
The student identifies the problem. This includes:
    a. Gathering information about the problem
    b. Identifying what needs to be solved and why
    c. Identifying constraints that must be addressed in a solution

Performance Ratings
Excellent: The student's work comprehensively includes all key aspects of the criterion (a-c) that apply.
Satisfactory: The student's work includes all key aspects of the criterion (a-c) that apply, but with some minor omissions and/or errors in the development of problem identification.
Needs Improvement: The student's work includes all key aspects of the criterion (a-c) that apply, with some major omissions and/or errors in the development of problem identification. However, there is an indication that the student has a general comprehension of what needs to be solved.
Unsatisfactory: The student's work omits one or more key aspects of the criterion (a-c) that apply. These omissions would make an accurate identification of the problem highly unlikely.

Exhibit 2. Criterion 2, Inquiry, Clayton State College

Information Identification
The student identifies relevant information about the work(s), object(s), and/or situation(s) under consideration. This involves:
   a. Identifying or recognizing significant and relevant information
   b. Distinguishing important and relevant from less important and irrelevant information
   c. Including information of appropriate depth and scope

Performance Ratings
Excellent: The student's work comprehensively includes all key aspects of the criterion (a-c) that apply.
Satisfactory: The student's work includes all key aspects of the criterion (a-c) that apply, but with some minor omissions and/or errors in the development of information identification.
Needs Improvement: The student's work includes all key aspects of the criterion (a-c) that apply, with some major omissions and/or errors in the development of information identification. However, there is an indication that the student has a general comprehension of the information needed for the inquiry.
Unsatisfactory: The student's work omits one or more key aspects of the criterion (a-c) that apply. These omissions would make a comprehensive identification of relevant information unlikely.

As noted, initial instruction deals with the cognitive process skills and is provided by a separate course emphasizing the procedures to follow when using these skills. Beginning in the fall of 1988, every other course in the curriculum will build on the foundation provided by the critical thinking course through instruction in and assessment of either inquiry or problem solving/decision making, or both.

Xavier University of Louisiana. At Xavier, two summer sessions are offered in critical thinking. One, called SOAR (Stress On Analysis Reasoning), is offered as preparation for students intending to major in the natural sciences. In this session, problem-solving skills are developed and practiced on exercises taken from such tests as the SAT and the ACT. Reading passages with accompanying questions are given to the student. The problem-solving steps are explained and then, in small groups, students work toward answering the questions. In subsequent science courses during the freshman and sophomore years, students continue the development of their problem-solving skills. At this level, students practice these skills on questions from such tests as the GRE and medical and dental school admission tests. Small groups composed of both SOAR alumni and other students work to develop one set of answers to the problem-solving questions.

An additional facet of Xavier's instruction in analytical reasoning in science is the reversal of the usual "lecture first, then lab" format of science instruction. In each segment of a science course, students work first in the laboratory. Using the scientific method of discovery, students begin with a situation, recognize a problem, decide on a procedure for solving the problem, gather data, hypothesize, and test for verification.

Xavier emphasizes both verbal and problem-solving skills, both in SOAR and in freshman and sophomore mathematics and science courses. There are weekly requirements for and testing of the student's growth in general and scientific vocabulary. Spokesmen for Xavier emphasize that problem-solving abilities are of little use if students cannot read scientific texts.

In the second of the summer sessions, EXCEL, Xavier attempts to prepare students intending to major in the humanities and the social sciences. Three hours are set aside in the morning for instruction and exercises aiming at the development of four skills: the abilities to create and vary perspective (that is, look at a problem from all sides), recognize assumptions and constraints, formulate and test hypotheses, and recognize the value assumptions inherent in data. These morning periods concentrate on the use of these abilities in philosophy, history, English, argumentation/debate, and sociology. In the afternoon, another three-hour period continues the use of these skills, first in answering test questions measuring verbal and quantitative skills, and then in writing. The thinking skills developed in EXCEL have not yet been systematically reinforced in subsequent college courses.

Both of these summer sessions, described as resembling honors courses, enroll students accepted for college-level work. The positive results of these summer sessions have been increases in student retention rates and SAT scores. Surveys also indicate increased student understanding and appreciation of the skills learned in these seminars (Kleinhaus, Carmichael, and Beattie, personal communication, 1987).

Conclusion

The individual and institutional approaches described in this chapter all serve the goal of improving the critical thinking of students. However, all of them may not be relevant to a particular institution's or faculty member's purpose in teaching and assessing critical thinking. Some common features emerge, though, that can guide practice in this area. First, an assessment to determine students' abilities in critical thinking can be administered upon entrance into the course or program, as a baseline for teaching and assessment. Next, separate courses emphasizing cognitive process skills can be offered to provide initial instruction and systematic assessment of critical thinking. Then, later assessments can be administered to certify that students have maintained or improved their critical thinking abilities during their programs of study. A graduation assessment may also be appropriate. Finally, faculty development workshops to ensure campuswide understanding of an agreement on the institution's view of critical thinking are helpful as faculty integrate the assessment of critical thinking into courses across the curriculum.

References

Banta, T. W., and Fisher, H. S. "Assessing Outcomes: The Real Value-Added Is in the Process." *Proceedings from the Conference on Legislative Action and Assessment: Reason and Reality.* Fairfax, Va.: George Mason University, 1986.

Beyer, B. K. *Practical Strategies for the Teaching of Thinking.* Boston: Allyn & Bacon, 1987.

Bloom, B. S. (ed.). *Taxonomy of Educational Objectives: The Classification of Educational Goals.* Vol. 1. *Cognitive Domain.* New York: McKay, 1956.

Clayton State College. *Critical Thinking Outcome Council.* Morrow, Ga.: Clayton State College, 1985.

Costa, A. L. "Thinking: How Do We Know Students Are Getting Better at It?" Roeper Review, 1984, *6,* 197–198.

Ennis, R. H. "Goals for a Critical Thinking Curriculum." In A. L. Costa (ed.), *Developing Minds: A Resource Book for Teaching Thinking.* Alexandria, Va.: Association for Supervision and Curriculum Development, 1985a.

Ennis, R. H. "Tests That Could Be Called Critical Thinking Tests." In A. L. Costa (ed.), *Developing Minds: A Resource Book for Teaching Thinking.* Alexandria, Va.: Association for Supervision and Curriculum Development, 1985b.

Ennis, R. H. "Critical Thinking Testing and Evaluation: Status, Issues, Needs." Paper presented at the 1986 annual meeting of the American Educational Research Association, San Francisco, April 1, 1986.

Ennis, R. H. "A Taxonomy of Critical Thinking Dispositions and Abilities." In J. B. Baron and R. J. Sternberg (eds.), *Teaching for Thinking.* New York: Freeman, 1987.

Hammerbacher, G. H. "Critical Thinking Assessment Criteria." Unpublished manuscript, King's College, 1987.

Loacker, G., Cromwell, L., Fey, J., and Rutherford, D. *Analysis and Communication at Alverno: An Approach to Critical Thinking.* Milwaukee, Wisc.: Alverno Productions, 1984.

McPeck, J. E. *Critical Thinking and Education.* Oxford, England: Martin Robertson, 1981.

Meyers, C. *Teaching Students to Think Critically: A Guide for Faculty in All Disciplines.* San Francisco: Jossey-Bass, 1986.

Segal, J. W., Chipman, S. F., and Glaser, R. (eds.). *Thinking and Learning Skills.* Vol. 1. *Relating Instruction to Research.* Hillsdale, N.J.: Erlbaum, 1985.

Smith, T. B. "The Uses of Assessment for Decision Making: A Primer about Northeast Missouri State University's Value-Added Program." *Proceedings from the Conference on Legislative Action and Assessment: Reason and Reality.* Fairfax, Va.: George Mason University, 1986.

Sternberg, R. J. "How Can We Teach Intelligence?" *Educational Leadership,* 1984, *48,* 38–48.

Sternberg, R. J. *Critical Thinking: Its Nature, Measurement, and Improvement.* In F. R. Link (ed.), *Essays of Intellect.* Alexandria, Va.: Association for Supervision and Curriculum Development, 1985.

Whimbey, A. "Teaching Sequential Thought: The Cognitive Skills Approach." *Phi Delta Kappan,* 1977, *59,* 255–259.

Whimbey, A., and Lochhead, J. *Problem Solving and Comprehension.* (3rd ed.) Philadelphia: The Franklin Press, 1982.

Young, R. E. (ed.). *Fostering Critical Thinking.* New Directions for Teaching and Learning, no. 3. San Francisco: Jossey-Bass, 1980.

C. Blaine Carpenter is professor of biology and James C. Doig is professor of philosophy at Clayton State College, Morrow, Georgia. They are members of the development team for Clayton's outcome-focused, assessment-based general education curriculum. The authors are also coordinators of the American Association of Higher Education's Critical Thinking Action Community.

Writing assignments are an effective means of assessment that can improve learning and teaching in any discipline.

Assessing Writing: Theory and Practice

Karen L. Greenberg

Writing is a powerful tool for stimulating thinking and learning. The act of writing enables students to explore their thoughts and feelings, to analyze their observations, and to clarify their understandings of new ideas. Recently, more college teachers have begun to incorporate writing in their daily classroom activities, and they are beginning to acknowledge that writing is not only central to learning but also a very effective form of evaluation.

The Importance of Assessing Writing

Writing is the consummate learning tool because it enables us to give coherent linguistic shape and order to the myriad fragments of perceptions, information, and ideas that we hear and see. Many teachers and researchers have noted the importance of writing as a medium for exploring information and synthesizing knowledge in disciplines across the curriculum (Freisinger, 1980; Fulwiler and Young, 1982; Maimon, 1982; McCrimmon, 1976; Newkirk and Atwell, 1982; Odell, 1980; Walvoord and Smith, 1982). Flower and Hayes (1981, 1984) stress the uniqueness of writing as a problem-solving strategy that enables people to concretize and explore nonverbal representations of meaning. Emig (1977) points

J. H. McMillan (ed.). *Assessing Students' Learning.*
New Directions for Teaching and Learning, no. 34. San Francisco: Jossey-Bass, Summer 1988.

out that "writing represents a unique mode of learning—not merely valuable, not merely special, but unique" (p. 122). Berthoff (1978) adds that "the work of the active mind is seeing relationships, finding forms, making meanings: When we write, we are doing in a particular way what we are already doing when we make sense of the world" (p. 12).

All of us who write understand the close connections between thinking, writing, and reasoning, whether we do our writing on paper, at the blackboard, or at the keyboard. By writing down thoughts, feelings, and ideas, we give them shape and logic; we open them to inspection and introspection. Competent writers use writing to acquire knowledge and to reflect on it. They also use writing to fulfill a variety of personal and social goals (to convey emotions, to entertain, to present information, and to convince or persuade). This ability to use writing to solidify and expand one's knowledge, experience, and observations is crucial to academic and professional success.

The value of writing as a means of facilitating learning is becoming more familiar to teachers across the curriculum, thanks to the growing number of publications on the topic (including Griffin, 1982). However, many teachers hesitate to assign writing because they are unsure of how to respond to it and because they fear being overwhelmed by stacks of lengthy papers. But by not assigning writing, teachers are missing unique opportunities to get important feedback on the effectiveness of their curriculum and instruction. Even more problematic is teachers' heavy reliance on multiple-choice quizzes and fill-in exams to assess students' command of course content and to determine their final grades. The majority of multiple-choice and fill-in tests assess the lowest level of learning—recognition—and do not measure coherent thought and expression of that thought. It is difficult for teachers to help students develop clear thinking and reasoning if they never look at some overt manifestation of their students' thought processes. By reading students' writing, faculty can discover students' reactions to and understanding of the concepts and principles under study. By assigning and assessing writing tasks, faculty can evaluate students' abilities to think in the language and the logic of their disciplines.

Fundamental Strategies for Assessing Writing

Teachers in any discipline can assign writing for a variety of assessment purposes. The most common objective in assessing writing at the beginning of a course is to gauge students' writing skills. Although content-area courses at many schools have writing prerequisites, these prerequisites do not guarantee that students will enter courses with a common level of writing mastery. By gaining a sense of the range of prose that students entering a course can actually produce, teachers can plan appropriate reading and writing activities for the course and can arrange extra help for students who need it. Diagnostic writing samples need not be lengthy or elaborate, nor do they have to be graded. One example of this type of assignment is a brief writing sample in which students introduce themselves to the teacher and explain what they expect to learn in the course. Another is a brief summary of the previous day's class lecture and discussion.

Diagnostic writing samples provide many insights into students' ability to accomplish the work of a particular course, insights that are not necessarily course-specific. For example, in order to function effectively in most undergraduate and graduate courses, students must be able to do the following writing tasks:

- Select and limit a subject
- Formulate and clarify ideas
- Develop a logical way of organizing ideas
- Locate and synthesize adequate supporting material
- Create and evaluate rhetorical structures appropriate to the subject and readers
- Make paragraphs coherent
- Adapt syntax to fit intended purpose and readers
- Adapt diction to fit intended purpose and readers
- Edit the writing to conform to the conventions of academic use and mechanics
- Document any citations or references according to the appropriate style manual.

These tasks are integral to the production of an effective piece of writing in any discipline. They can be assessed through writing samples and evaluation of these samples as shown in the grid of Figure 1. The writing tasks and skills summarized in Figure 1 can be used to assess almost any type of academic writing. Additional discipline- or course-specific skills can be added to the grid in order to assess students' mastery of the intellectual strategies and the language of the discipline. These skills—and some procedures used to assess them—are discussed in the section that follows.

Procedures for Assessing Writing Across the Curriculum

Although teachers often perceive writing assessment as a subjective, idiosyncratic matter, recent advances in writing assessment have shown that it is possible to make valid, reliable judgments about students' writing skills. Currently, the measure preferred by most writing programs and writing teachers for assessing writers' competence or mastery is a holistically scored *writing sample*. Scoring a sample of writing enables a teacher to assess a student's ability to shape a response to a topic—to

Figure 1. Criteria for Assessing General Writing Skills

Writing Task	Done Effectively	Needs Some Revision	Needs Extensive Revision
Limit a subject			
Clarify ideas			
Organize ideas			
Coherently develop ideas			
Provide and effectively synthesize supporting material			
Create and evaluate rhetorical structures appropriate to subject and readers			
Fit syntax to intended purpose and readers			
Fit diction to intended purpose and readers			
Make writing conform to conventions of academic use and mechanics			

compose, revise, and edit. Moreover, writing samples allow teachers to assess writing proficiency over a wide range of tasks, tasks that parallel the kinds of writing expected in academia and in the workplace. Assessing samples of students' writing also sends the message that writing means developing and revising an extended piece of discourse, not filling in blanks in exercise workbooks or on computer screens.

Just about any writing task assigned in an academic course can be used for assessment purposes. Essay tests are traditional, but other assignments may be more appropriate for a particular course—assignments such as "microthemes" (Work, 1979), lab reports, responses to readings, summaries of class discussions, letters to the editor, and case studies or analyses. Indeed, Anderson and others (1983) argue that short assignments provide many benefits for students and teachers alike: "Several short assignments instead of one or two long ones allow for incremental learning of content, and whatever comments you make about the presentation of ideas can serve writers on the *next* try, where they can apply your suggestions in a new context" (p. 37). Moreover, several brief writing samples enable teachers to assess students' abilities to write for a variety of specific readers and specific purposes. (For suggestions on developing and implementing different types of writing assignments, see also Fulwiler, 1982; Fulwiler and Jones, 1982; and Maimon and others, 1981.)

Holistic Scoring. Writing samples, whether brief or lengthy, should be scored holistically. Holistic scoring is a system based on the response of a concerned reader to a meaningful whole piece of writing. The reader evaluates the piece of writing as a unit of expression, rather than as a series of isolated skills (White, 1985, p. 18). Holistic scoring has three strengths: It enables a teacher to articulate and employ clear, specific criteria; it focuses on what writers have done well (as opposed to focusing on their errors); and it allows teachers to share their evaluative criteria with each other and with students. Typically, when a teacher scores a writing sample holistically, he or she rates it according to a scoring scale or guide that describes responses at different levels of competence. Most holistic scoring guides use a five- or six-point scale. Exhibit 1 is a sample holistic scoring guide.

Evaluative Grid Scoring. Another way to assess students' writing samples is to use the evaluative grid depicted in Figure 1, adding discipline- or course-specific skills. Descriptions of these skills can be general or specific, depending on the teacher's concerns. For example, here are some general evaluative criteria for effective academic writing:

- The writing retells or reports events or experiences in a clear, logical manner
- It develops new generalizations or hypotheses from existing reports and data
- It predicts the probable outcome of a new set of circumstances, on the basis of existing reports and data
- It analyzes concepts and/or relationships clearly
- It synthesizes anecdotes, opinions, facts, data, and interpretations logically and clearly
- It explicates a viewpoint and provides convincing supporting evidence.

Here are some specific evaluative criteria for effective writing in different disciplines:

- It balances the writer's emotional and intellectual responses to a work (of art or of prose)
- It details the writer's perceptions of the parts of a work and the relationships among these parts
- It explains the significance of the writer's hypotheses
- It analyzes and integrates various competing theories for a behavior or a phenomenon
- It adequately describes all the methods used to collect data
- It explains the significance of any discrepancies from predicted results

- It balances summaries, paraphrases, and quotations
- It incorporates appropriate tables, charts, and graphs
- It presents information in a clear, straightforward, unembellished style, without relying too heavily on the passive voice
- It uses accurate and appropriate technical vocabulary, without incorporating imprecise jargon
- It uses the appropriate format for citing references within the text and at the end of the text.

Both methods—the holistic scoring scale and the evaluative grid—enable teachers to communicate their criteria to students and to provide focused, relevant responses rapidly and efficiently. In addition, both methods can be used by students to assess their own writing skills and development.

Portfolio System. Another method for assessing students' writing is the portfolio system, which requires students to keep a folder or portfolio of three or four pieces of writing, some of which is done in class and some of which is written and revised outside class. The number and types of pieces are determined by the teacher or by a departmental committee and can include the types of writing tasks that are most representative of the discipline. Teachers can collect portfolios at various points in the semester and respond with brief oral or written commentary to the enclosed pieces. Portfolio assessment is currently the sole method used to determine students' writing proficiency at SUNY-Stony Brook, and it seems to be working (Elbow and Belanoff, 1986). At Stony Brook, teachers collect portfolios at the middle and the end of the semester and give them to other teachers to grade on a pass/fail basis. This procedure makes teachers allies of their students, working with them to help them pass, and it makes teachers more conscious of their colleagues' standards and evaluative criteria.

The portfolio method of assessing writing has many more strengths than it does weaknesses (see Belanoff and Elbow, 1986, and Elbow and Belanoff, 1986). Its chief advantages over other types of writing assessment are that (1) it enables teachers to assess students' abilities to write different types of academic assignments, (2) it allows teachers to evaluate students' revising skills, and (3) it encourages collaboration among students and among teachers. Most important, portfolio assessment enables teachers to intervene in students' writing processes and determine where they need additional assistance.

Peer Group and Self-Evaluation. Two other methods for assessing writing are peer group evaluation and self-evaluation. Students can learn to evaluate one another's writings and to provide useful feedback using response guides like the one illustrated in Exhibit 2. They can also use revision checklists, like the one illustrated in Exhibit 3, to evaluate their own writing. (See Beaven, 1977, for additional procedures to help students evaluate their own writing and the writing of their classmates.)

Exhibit 1. Sample Holistic Scoring Guide

6: A paper in this category will complete all the tasks set by the assignment. It will be distinguished by lucid and orderly thinking—and may even introduce an original interpretation of the writing topic. It will be virtually free from errors in mechanics, usage, and sentence structure. And there will be evidence of superior control of language.

5: A paper in this category may slight, but not ignore, one of the tasks of the assignment or deal with it only by implication, but the writer will demonstrate a clear understanding to the writing topic. It may not be as thoughtful or as carefully reasoned as a 6 paper, but it will not be characterized by mere statement and restatement of ideas at a high level of generality. Although the paper may have minor weaknesses in paragraphing, it will contain evidence of the writer's ability to organize information into unified and coherent units. It will be largely free from serious errors in mechanics, usage, and sentence structure. And it will be generally well written, characterized by clarity if not by felicity of expression.

4: Although a paper in this category may execute the assignment less completely or less systematically than a 6 or 5 paper does, the paper will come to terms with the basic tasks of the assignment. The reasoning may be less precise and less discriminating than one would expect to find in a 6 or 5 paper, but it will not be flawed by logical fallacies. It may insufficiently develop a point or two, but it will give evidence of the writer's ability to support key ideas. It will be organized and paragraphed well enough to allow the reader to move with relative ease through the discourse, though there may be some disjointedness and lack of focus. It may contain errors in mechanics, usage, and sentence structure, but not so frequently as to call into question the writer's command of the conventions of the standard dialect or to consistently distract the reader from the content. The paper will display generally accurate use of language.

3: A paper will fall into this category if it shows serious difficulty managing the tasks of the assignment; OR if it shows definite weaknesses in analytic thinking; OR if the paper is so markedly underdeveloped that key ideas stand virtually without illustration; OR if errors in sentence structure, usage, and mechanics seriously interfere with readability. There may be distinctive weaknesses in paragraphing and organization, but the total effect will not be chaotic. The writer's control of language may be uncertain.

2: A paper in this category may fail to come to terms with the assignment; that is, tasks may be ignored, misconstrued, badly mishandled, or redefined to accommodate what the writer wants to say or is able to say. There is also likely to be a combination of the following defects: serious errors in reasoning, little or no development of ideas, and no clear progression from one part to the next. There may be serious and frequent errors in sentence structure, usage, and mechanics, giving the impression of distinctly inferior writing.

1: This category is reserved for the paper in which a combination of errors, conceptual confusion, and disorganization creates the impression of ineptitude. There are, however, definite indications of the writer's attempt to deal with the topic.

0: This paper is obviously "off-topic" by intention, whatever its writing quality.

Source: White, 1985, pp. 135-136.

Exhibit 2. Sample Student Feedback Guide

1. Get into a group of two or three students and take turns reading your first drafts aloud to one another. When it is your turn to read, speak slowly and clearly, and do not interrupt your reading with comments about the draft.
2. When it is your turn to listen to a classmate, put your draft away where you cannot see it. Try not to think about your draft; instead, concentrate on your classmate's draft. Listen closely to each classmate and try to understand the ideas that each is trying to communicate. Do *not* write while your classmate is reading. Do not judge classmates' writing or make any criticisms.
3. After each person reads his or her draft, you have three minutes to take notes on what you have heard. Write down what you think were the author's main points and important details. Write down any words or phrases that you remember clearly. Also write down any point or sentence that seemed particularly interesting or that you want to know more about.
4. After everyone in the group finishes reading and writing, take turns reading what you have written about each person's draft.
5. When it is your turn to listen to your classmates' responses, take out your draft and write notes on it. Note the ideas, sentences, or words that your classmates point out, and note the places where they may have misunderstood you or where they want more information.

Exhibit 3. Sample Student Self-Evaluation Questions

1. What are the strengths of this essay? Which parts need to be made more forceful and convincing?
2. What is the point of each paragraph? In the margin next to each paragraph, write a sentence explaining what it should make the reader think, feel, or do. If the paragraph does not do what you intended it to do, add new ideas or rewrite the original ones.
3. Is one of your supporting sentences actually the main point that you want to make? If so, rewrite the essay so that is focuses on and supports its new main point.
4. Are your details specific enough? Do the details convey clear pictures of how your subject looks and sounds to you? If not, cross out vague words and add descriptive words and active verbs.
5. How does each observation, experience, fact, or number support the main idea of each paragraph? If you are not sure whether it does, cross it out or rewrite it so that it is clearly related to main point.
6. Do you think your reader will believe your observations and direct experiences? If not, consult sources and add more supporting details and data and cite their sources.
7. Does the introduction make your main point(s) clear? Is it interesting? If not, use a different technique to develop a new introduction or make the original one clearer and more interesting.
8. Does the conclusion remind the reader of the main point(s), without using the same words you used in the introduction? Does it stick to the point, without bringing up new ideas? If not, make the conclusion clearer and more to the point, or develop a new one using a different technique.

Procedures for Using Writing to Assess Learning

Another purpose for assigning and evaluating writing is to assess students' learning. Teachers can use writing samples to assess students' understanding of course goals or objectives, to assess their mastery of course content and evaluate their progress as learners, and to get information on the effectiveness of curricula and instruction. By evaluating writing, teachers can discover how much the student knows and needs to know, and they can find out how well they have taught what has been learned and how to structure successive learning experiences in the course. Writing may be the best classroom assessment activity for supporting the conditions necessary for effective learning: active involvement in the subject, self-defined strategies for integrating knowledge, and opportunities for timely and relevant feedback.

In his review of recent research on writing and learning, Applebee (1984) concludes that "the more a writer must manipulate new material in the process of writing about it, the better that writer will come to understand that material" (p. 586). This conclusion is supported by other researchers: Milton (1982) says, "At least one clear conclusion emerges (and is supported by other studies); students who prepare to take essay tests outperform students who prepare to take other type tests. Of major importance is the fact that the superiority lasts over a period of time" (p. 35).

Assessing Cognitive Learning. At the beginning of the semester, teachers can assign brief essays exploring students' ideas about course objectives and about their current knowledge of the material that will be considered in a course. These enable teachers to determine what students already know about course topics, what they want to learn, and what they think the course will explore. A classroom discussion of these essays will clarify students' misunderstandings about the course. Moreover, by helping students understand the goals, demands, and deadlines of the course, teachers are encouraging them to make a commitment to the work of the course.

Writing assignments are also practical tools for assessing students' mastery of course content, evaluating their progress as learners, and getting information on the effectiveness of curricula and instruction. Writing can be assigned spontaneously at any appropriate moment in a lesson in order to determine if students understand concepts and relationships. By asking students to process information in writing—to analyze information and use it to accomplish a goal—teachers can evaluate students' understanding of the material and can see students' minds at work on problems.

The intellectual demands of writing usually exceed those of other forms of assessment. Multiple-choice and fill-in exams typically provide information about students' ability to memorize and recall new principles and concepts; rarely do they demonstrate students' ability to apply, analyze, synthesize, and evaluate new ideas and information. From students' writing, teachers can determine the extent to which students can interpret and express what they have learned and the implications and consequences of their knowledge. In the seminal *Taxonomy of Educational Objectives* (Bloom, 1956), almost all the tasks (pp. 149–200) recommended for testing the more "complex" cognitive objectives of learning (analysis, synthesis, and evaluation) are writing tasks. Indeed, these tasks are still excellent examples of writing assignments for assessing students' understanding of course content.

One popular technique for assessing students' mastery of course content is the microtheme assignment. A microtheme is an essay brief enough to be typed on a five-by-eight index card and organized according to a very specific format (Work, 1979). Microthemes can be used successfully in both small and large classes; students are given the assignment and a description of the criteria by which the theme will be evaluated. Not all microthemes need be graded, and those that are can be scored rapidly with a simple rating scale. Other options for responding to microthemes include writing brief comments on them and/or duplicating and discussing several of the most effective and least effective ones. (See Bean, Drenk, and Lee, 1982, for examples of microtheme assignments and scoring procedures.)

Assessing Affective Learning. Writing assignments are valuable not only for assessing students' cognitive skills but also for evaluating the affective goals of learning. Most teachers hope that students will learn certain attitudes toward the phenomena and strategies of their disciplines and will internalize certain values. Checklists and questionnaires can be used to determine students' reactions to materials and commitment to different values, but writing assignments provide a more comprehensive picture of the internalization of values. For example, in their handbook of formative and summative evaluation of learning, Bloom, Hastings, and Madaus (1971) offer an example of an essay assignment that can be used to determine the extent to which students have internalized certain values about mathematics. Students are given the following quote: "No music nor [sic] poem, no other work of art gives me a greater sense of the beauty of harmony than a well developed body of mathematical doctrine, and I cannot avoid the feeling that there are many people who are able in some measure to add the same pleasure to their life" (p. 235). Students can write essays about their responses to this quote, or they can write their "opinion[s] on the importance of mathematics in our life" (Bloom, Hastings, and Madaus, 1971, p. 235). This enables them to express the why and wherefores of their opinions of the value and elegance of mathematics.

Writing assignments, moreover, can demonstrate the ways in which students approach problems, decide what they see as the important elements, and solve problems in terms of issues, evidence, and consequences, rather than in terms of dogmatic precepts or wishful thinking. In their work on values and teaching, Raths, Harmin, and Simon (1966, pp. 28–30) delineate many writing assignments that allow students to explore their beliefs, examine alternative options, and consider the consequences of specific beliefs and actions. Writing about their beliefs and values helps students clarify them and become more actively committed to them; writing is an excellent medium for relating ethical standards and personal value judgments.

Summary

Writing activities make significant contributions to the development of higher-level cognitive and affective skills. By assigning and assessing students' writing, faculty can evaluate students' responses to and understanding of the concepts, logic, and language of their disciplines. Teachers need not be experts on writing or on assessment to respond to students' ideas and logic and to the effectiveness of their writing. All they need is to be committed to helping students become active learners willing to explore facts, feelings, values, and ideas in writing.

References

Anderson, J., Eisenberg, N., Holland, J., and Wiener, H. *Integrated Skills Reinforcement: Reading, Writing, Speaking, and Listening Across the Curriculum.* New York: Longman, 1983.

Applebee, A. "Writing and Reasoning." *Review of Educational Research,* 1984, *54* (4), 577–596.

Bean, J. C., Drenk, D., and Lee, F. D. "Microtheme Strategies for Developing Cognitive Skills." In C. W. Griffin (ed.), *Teaching Writing in All Disciplines.* New Directions for Teaching and Learning, no. 12. San Francisco: Jossey-Bass, 1982.

Beaven, M. "Individualized Goal Setting, Self-Evaluation, and Peer Evaluation." In C. R. Cooper and L. Odell (eds.), *Evaluating Writing: Describing, Measuring, Judging.* Urbana, Ill.: National Council of Teachers of English, 1977.

Belanoff, P., and Elbow, P. "Using Portfolios to Increase Collaboration and Community in a Writing Program." *Writing Program Administration,* 1986, *9* (3), 27–40.

Berthoff, A. *Forming, Thinking, Writing: The Composing Imagination.* Rochelle Park, N.J.: Hayden, 1978.

Bloom, B. S. (ed.). *Taxonomy of Educational Objectives: The Classification of Educational Goals.* Vol. 1. *Cognitive Domain.* New York: McKay, 1956.

Bloom, B., Hastings, J. T., and Madaus, G. *Handbook on Formative and Summative Evaluation of Student Learning.* New York: McGraw-Hill, 1971.

Elbow, P., and Belanoff, P. "Using Portfolios to Judge Writing Proficiency at

58

SUNY–Stony Brook." In P. Connally and T. Vilardi (eds.), *New Developments in College Writing Programs.* New York: Modern Language Association, 1986.

Emig, J. "Writing as a Mode of Learning." *College Composition and Communication,* 1977, *28,* 122–128.

Flower, L., and Hayes, J. R. "A Cognitive Process Theory of Writing." *College Composition and Communication,* 1981, *32,* 365–387.

Flower, L., and Hayes, J. R. "Images, Plans, and Prose: The Representation of Meaning in Writing." *Written Communication,* 1984, *1* (1), 120–160.

Freisinger, R. "Cross-Disciplinary Writing Workshops: Theory and Practice." *College English,* 1980, *42* (2), 154–166.

Fulwiler, T. "Writing: An Act of Cognition." In C. W. Griffin (ed.), *Teaching Writing in All Disciplines.* New Directions for Teaching and Learning, no. 12. San Francisco: Jossey-Bass, 1982.

Fulwiler, T., and Jones, R. "Assigning and Evaluating Transactional Writing." In T. Fulwiler and A. Young (eds.), *Language Connections: Writing and Reading Across the Curriculum.* Urbana, Ill.: National Council of Teachers of English, 1982.

Fulwiler, T., and Young, A. (eds.). *Language Connections: Writing and Reading Across the Curriculum.* Urbana, Ill.: National Council of Teachers of English, 1982.

Griffin, C. W. (ed.). *Teaching Writing in All Disciplines.* New Directions for Teaching and Learning, no. 12. San Francisco: Jossey-Bass, 1982.

McCrimmon, J. M. "Writing as a Way of Knowing." In J. M. McCrimmon (ed.), *The Promise of English.* Urbana, Ill.: National Council of Teachers of English, 1976.

Maimon, E. "Writing Across the Curriculum: Past, Present, and Future." In C. W. Griffin (ed.), *Teaching Writing in All Disciplines.* New Directions for Teaching and Learning, no. 12. San Francisco: Jossey-Bass, 1982.

Maimon, E., Belcher, G., Hearn, G., Nodine, B., and O'Connor, F. *Writing in the Arts and Sciences.* Cambridge, Mass.: Winthrop, 1981.

Milton, O. *Will That Be on the Final?* Springfield, Ill.: Thomas, 1982.

Newkirk, T., and Atwell, N. (eds.). *Understanding Writing: Ways of Observing, Learning, and Teaching.* Chelmsford, Mass.: Northeast Regional Exchange, 1982.

Odell, L. "The Process of Writing and the Process of Learning." *College Composition and Communication,* 1980, *31,* 42–50.

Raths, L., Harmin, M., and Simon, S. *Values and Teaching: Working with Values in the Classroom.* Columbus, Ohio: Merrill, 1966.

Walvoord, B., and Smith, H. "Coaching the Process of Writing." In C. W. Griffin (ed.), *Teaching Writing in All Disciplines.* New Directions for Teaching and Learning, no. 12. San Francisco: Jossey-Bass, 1982.

White, E. *Teaching and Assessing Writing: Recent Advances in Understanding, Evaluating, and Improving Student Performance.* San Francisco: Jossey-Bass, 1985.

Work, J. C. "Reducing Three Papers to Ten: A Method for Literature Courses." In G. Stanford (ed.), *How to Handle the Paper Load: Classroom Practices in Teaching English.* Urbana, Ill.: National Council of Teachers of English, 1979.

Karen L. Greenberg is associate professor of English at Hunter College of The City University of New York, where she teaches composition and linguistics courses and directs the college's Writing Center. She is also project director of the National Testing Network in Writing and a member of the executive committee of the Conference on College Composition and Communication.

*Assessing adults' experiential learning for college credit is
gaining academic credibility as more systematic ways of setting
standards and measuring learning are demonstrated.*

Assessing Experiential Learning

Susan Simosko

During the past twenty years, students over the age of twenty-five have
become the fastest-growing group of college students. Today more than
one out of every three enrolled students is over twenty-five. Many of these
students arrive on campus already rich in experience and learning. Unlike
many of their younger counterparts, they come with a strong sense of
purpose and a desire to acquire new skills and knowledge that will enable
them to move on in their lives—to new jobs, promotions within existing
ones, or better credentials that will give them future confidence and flexibility. Often unable to commit themselves to four or more years of full-
time study, and unwilling to opt for the seven or more years that would
be necessary to earn a baccalaureate degree part-time, they are increasingly seeking ways of having their college-level learning acknowledged
and accredited. They have neither time nor the inclination to repeat the
learning that they have already acquired. Work (both paid and unpaid),
avocations, job and military training, and independent reading all provide rich opportunities for learning away from the college classroom. It
is this experiential learning for which adults seek credit.

Learning, Not Experience, Is the Key

It is not experience that is assessed for credit, but rather the learning people obtain from that experience. The term *experiential learning*

J. H. McMillan (ed.). *Assessing Students' Learning.*
New Directions for Teaching and Learning, no. 34. San Francisco: Jossey-Bass, Summer 1988.

legitimately describes most of the learning that occurs throughout our lives. In this chapter, *experiential learning* is defined as learning that has reached a level of competence in a particular skill or knowledge domain through direct contact with what is studied or practiced in a particular college course. Such learning often begins unintentionally; that is, we may not be studying or practicing in the formal sense of these words. Rather, learning may begin by chance—something catches our attention or needs doing or prompts us to seek answers to questions we have never thought to ask. With this initial impetus, we begin to explore new areas of learning in our personal, professional, or avocational lives, and we grow to achieve new skills, knowledge, or understanding.

Sometimes, of course, the focus of our learning is very intentional: We take a training course offered by our employer, enroll in an adult education course, or hire a tutor to help us speak French. Adults seeking to have their experiential learning assessed want recognition and credit for both kinds of achievement.

While experiential learning has long been acknowledged as intrinsic to the human experience, the assessment of it for college credit in the United States is a relatively recent phenomenon (Chickering, 1977). Yet today in the United States, there are over 1,200 colleges and universities offering adults the opportunity to earn college credit for college-level learning acquired away from the college classroom ("Opportunities for Credit," 1986). Thousands of credits are being awarded for this learning each year by the full range of accredited collegiate institutions.

Assessment of Learning from Experience Expands

Institutional and foundation support has contributed significantly to the spread and acceptance of experiential learning over the past twenty years. The W. K. Kellogg Foundation, the Ford Foundation, and the Carnegie Foundation, among others, have all contributed to support the development of assessment opportunities for adults, through such programs as the College-Level Examination Program (CLEP) of the College Board, and the research and programs of the Council for Adult and Experiential Learning (CAEL) and its member institutions.

In recent years there has been a significant increase in the kinds of areas that are assessed for credit and, therefore, in the kinds of students who are being encouraged to use the various credit-bearing options. No longer do people come seeking recognition only for learning in traditional liberal arts or business areas. As Dewees (in press) has said, the 1980s have seen a vast increase in the number of individuals requesting assessment of their skills and knowledge in technical subjects. With the deindustrialization of the American economy, skilled technical workers have begun to find certain job markets closed or extremely competitive.

As in any tight job market, credentials become important, and employers begin to select their employees on the basis of such formal credentials as college degrees. This has been a trend of the past decade. Colleges have responded by developing curricula and credentials for many trades that formerly were learned on the job during some form of workplace apprenticeship. A number of assessment programs for prior learning have emerged to enable the new worker-students to earn credit for their past achievements while working toward credentials that will strengthen their job possibilities for the future.

The movement to accredit prior learning is no longer limited to the United States. During the past three years, for example, rapid advances have been made in Quebec. Under government mandate, the province has implemented prior learning assessment programs among the forty-four colleges of the Fédération des Cegeps, the strong network of French- and English-based colleges most similar in academic offerings to United States community colleges. In Great Britain, work begun in the polytechnics is being extended to the education colleges, business and industry, and major government initiatives. Similarly, work is going forward in the Philippines, France, Australia, and many other nations. In each country, the reasons for accrediting adults' experiential learning are the same: There is a dire need to build on the strengths of individuals, identify their skills and abilities in the world economy, make better use of existing educational and training facilities, and support and encourage lifelong learners who will be able to contribute to their respective societies and communities throughout their lifetimes.

Defining Experiential Learning Outcomes

The natural tendency among college administrators and faculty who wish to develop programs designed to accredit adults' experiential or prior learning is to assume that it requires judgments separate from and different from those made about classroom-based learning. However, the assessment of prior learning involves the same kinds of academic judgments about what a student knows and can do. The process may be different, but the judgments are the same.

As in classroom practice, before such judgments can be made it is essential that the expected learning be defined and the criteria for success be clearly articulated. Unlike the classroom instructor, however, the assessor of experiential learning must focus only on the outcomes of the learning. Since he or she is not responsible for providing the instruction and has had no control over the manner or time in which the learning took place, the good assessor must consider the discipline or course matter as a whole and determine both what is most important and how best to assess those factors in the student's achievement. Most teachers at all levels of education are comfortable outlining the material to be covered or taught, and good practice in the assessment of experiential learning means defining as clearly as possible what students are expected to know and be able to do in relation to the subject matter of an established curriculum. This requires faculty experts or assessors to draw up statements of the expectations for a particular course or discipline. Known as learning outcome statements, these documents provide guidance not only to assessors but also to students, who must show that they really do possess the skills and knowledge they claim.

Defining the criteria for effective performance is the first of seven functions outlined by Reilly (1977) in a discussion of the role of the expert judge in the assessment of prior learning. Criteria are usually developed by small groups, and many faculty can contribute to defining such criteria in the form of learning outcome statements. These statements specify the knowledge, skills, and/or understandings that a person is expected to acquire in a given curriculum. The procedure enables both teacher and student to know in advance what is expected, regardless of the method of assessment. Typical learning outcomes might read as follows:

- The data-processing student should be able to create data file formats and output specifications
- The economics student should be able to explain, both orally and in writing, the basic tools used to measure the status of the nation's economy
- The music history student should be able to analyze and give concrete examples of nineteenth- and twentieth-century music.

Learning outcome statements relate to the expected achievement of the student, not to the method by which the learning was accomplished. This emphasis on outcomes may well be intrinsic to any educational or training initiative meant to ensure fair and reliable assessments, but it is absolutely crucial to the assessment of experiential learning because, again, such evaluations cannot be undertaken in light of any particular classroom experience.

Learning outcome statements have five essential characteristics (Cook, 1978). They should be unambiguous and readily understandable by both student and teacher; describe observable, demonstrable, and assessable performance; contain action verbs that have relatively few meanings; be broader in scope than specific tasks or skills; and be applicable to skills, knowledge, and understanding.

In every discipline, it is possible to define learning in terms of outcomes. Sometimes faculty see the relevance of this task to someone else's field but not their own, and they say that their own disciplines are too complex or not vocational enough, or that they themselves are satisfied with their own often undefinable ways of assessing student achievement. Nevertheless, an excellent learning outcome statement can frequently highlight the relevance of such statements to faculty's classroom work. By describing course content in learning outcome statements, faculty may improve as teachers and obtain better and more complete work from students. Learning outcome statements can also permit faculty to recognize individual differences in a way that was not possible before. Faculty may also feel more confident in assigning grades, as a result.

To write effective learning outcome statements, assessors must describe who is to exhibit the performance, what performance is to be exhibited, what conditions (if any) are to be provided for the learner at the time of the assessment, and what constitutes a minimally acceptable response.

Setting Standards

Judging the learning is another of the assessment functions identified by Reilly (1977). To do this, faculty need to set the standards for successful performance. How is this done? What approaches are there? One possible strategy can be borrowed from baseball: After a particularly exciting game, three umpires were in the dressing room discussing how they had made their calls. The first one said, "I call it like I see it." The second one said, "I call it like it is." The third one said, "What I call it makes it what it is." Each of these perspectives is real, and each represents a faculty perspective on making academic judgments. To see this, substitute three different faculty members. The first recognizes that what is being applied is an internalized standard, not explicit but reasonably consistent: "I grade it like I see it." The second perceives that the standard is universal, one that would be recognized and applied by all other competent colleagues in similar situations: "I grade it like it is." The third recognizes that in the absence of a precise universal standard, each decision on whether the learner has met the standard refines and further defines the standard itself: "What I grade it makes the standard."

As academic referees of experiential learning, we make decisions that are usually more complex and have greater impact on the lives of individuals, but the process is similar to the one that confronts the umpire. For most assessors, of course, setting standards is an amalgam of all three approaches, but, like umpires, assessors need to learn their jobs and strive to do them consistently and fairly over time. More often than not, decisions about learners need to be right and to elicit agreement among other experts on a regular basis.

Making the right decision for a given learner, however, requires that we know why we have set the standards we have. Are we concerned with content validity, predictive validity, or both? Do we want to know if the individual has certain skills, knowledge, and understanding? Do we want to be able to predict the future performance of the individual? To what extent are we interested both in recognizing what has already been achieved and in predicting what may be achieved in the future? These questions must be answered in the process of setting standards.

As in writing learning outcome statements, faculty find it easiest to draw on the combined strengths of a department or program to set criteria or standards together. Developing agreed-upon learning outcome statements and standards often leads to lively discussion and discourse on what is truly important in a given field. As teaching faculty, most of us have our own particular interests and strengths, those that are often emphasized in our teaching. In working toward group consensus, however, it is often necessary for some people to give up or modify their special interests. Most often, though, properly trained faculty aiming at a predefined goal are very surprised to see how quickly they can reach consensus on learning outcomes and standards.

Accurate and Fair Assessment

By defining the learning outcomes and standards for all courses or sets of competencies in a given discipline, we make it possible to assess individual performance and ability more efficiently and accurately, regardless of when, where, or under what circumstances the learning takes place. By assessing learning from experience, and in light of the expected outcomes and standards, we allow students to use the educational or training resources available to them. For example, a student may need to focus on the theory of a given subject, having already demonstrated competence in the applied area of the field, or vice versa. Or it may be that a student has a range of skills and competencies covering several courses but lacks the depth of understanding expected in each separate course. Knowing this enables students and their mentors, advisors, and teachers to make more rational educational decisions about a student's accomplishments and future educational needs.

Approaching experiential learning and its assessment from this perspective also enables us to evaluate as well as value the differing strengths individuals possess. No two people can or do know exactly the same things; in any given classroom, there is a range of student ability. Similarly, as we assess adults' prior learning, we witness a range of competence and ability. One of the most difficult concepts for faculty new to assessing experiential learning is the idea of the minimally competent student. In setting standards and making evaluations or recommendations—letter grades, or pass/fail options—we need to remember that in traditional college classroom evaluations, a grade of D still enables a person to go on to new work, often at a higher level. Why, then, should learners who have achieved at the same level through an alternative learning mode be held accountable to higher standards? In all cases, some students will know and be able to do a lot, and some only a little. In either situation, if learning outcome statements and standards are in place, there will be a firm basis on which to make rational judgments about each student.

Documenting Learning

Another of the crucial roles assessors play is to select the best assessment method for each student. It is essential that learning, not experience, be assessed and that students have the responsibility of conveying this learning, not just reiterating the experiences from which the learning was drawn.

Students can and do convey their learning in a variety of ways, but most commonly at colleges and universities students are expected to construct portfolios of their learning, documented portraits of what they know and can do. Generally speaking, the construction of a portfolio requires the student to go through four distinct, interrelated processes: identifying the learning, expressing the learning in terms of college-level curricula or competencies, relating it to overall educational and career objectives, and compiling the evidence or demonstrating the competence. Specific procedures vary from college to college, but most expect students to follow guidelines formed roughly around these four steps. Some colleges offer portfolio development courses or workshops to help students through the process; others provide self-instructional materials. Colleges generally provide counselors or advisors to give guidance and support to students beginning the process.

As described elsewhere (Simosko, 1985), students compile their portfolios in a variety of ways. Most commonly, they provide either direct or indirect evidence, or some combination of each. Direct evidence means products or performances actually produced by the student, such as poems, paintings, computer programs, dress designs, architectural drawings, written manuals, a videotape of the student dancing or playing a musical instrument, or an actual performance. Examples of indirect evidence may include a magazine review of the student's poems or paintings, a letter of verification from an employer attesting to the student's accomplishments in preparing company training manuals, the program notes of a concert in which the student performed, or photographs of completed dresses or buildings that the student claims to have designed. It is up to the assessor, in conjunction with the student, to determine the best way for the student to present evidence of the learning.

In some cases, students have no physical evidence of their learning. Consider, for example, the avid reader of Virginia Woolf. The student has read the primary works and many secondary sources but has never written a paper, given a lecture, or led a class discussion about some aspect of Woolf's work. Such a person would be an excellent candidate for prior learning assessment. In preparing for the assessment, the student could be asked to write a brief narrative or autobiographical statement, including an annotated bibliography of Woolf's work. On the basis of this information, the assessor might set up an interview with the student or ask him or her to write a paper on a particular topic or give an oral presentation on some aspect of the work.

There are other ways to assess students besides using the evidence they submit in portfolios. Faculty may undertake a product or performance assessment, design an interview or examination, or evaluate written material prepared by students. In all cases, however, the assessment process requires the use of expert judgment, and assessors must have ready access to students' work and to the students themselves, whether in person or by telephone.

It is important to maintain the integrity of each step in the evaluation process. In a product assessment, for example, the student's work needs to be directly linked to the learning outcomes and to the standards set for success in a particular course or set of courses. Some products may stand by themselves. For example, a set of poems published in *The New Yorker* may be sufficient evidence for earning credit in a creative writing course. An annual report prepared by the student may represent partial evidence of the student's learning in a business writing course. Additional products or materials may need to be supplied by the student or supplemented by other assessment procedures. Again, when the assessment is linked to specified learning outcomes and standards, the relevance and applicability of various products and performances becomes very clear.

This chapter has focused on assessing learning through specially designed assessment procedures, but there are other options. There are two well-known credit-by-examination programs, CLEP (already mentioned) and the ACT Proficiency Examination Program (PEP). These programs both provide useful and inexpensive ways for adults to seek credit for their prior learning. The tests cover a wide range of liberal arts, business, occupational, and technical areas and are administered several times a year across the country. There are also institutionally based credit-by-examination programs, many of which are used nationally. Those at Ohio University and at Thomas A. Edison State College are two of the more notable ones.

Many colleges also use the guidelines published by the American Council on Education (ACE) for awarding credit for training received in the military or through business and industry. Training courses in both domains are evaluated by college faculty under the auspices of ACE. Faculty recommend whether credit should be granted to someone satisfactorily completing the training program, and if so, how much credit. ACE publishes annual credit recommendation guides used by more than

1,000 colleges to grant credit. (Information about these guides may be obtained from ACE, One Dupont Circle, Washington, D.C. 20036.)

Faculty Training

Colleges and universities show considerable variation in the policies they develop for using the various methods of recognizing prior learning, but most recognize and accredit learning either for specific courses or for generic competencies. In either case, all institutions rely on the expert judgment of faculty or outside experts to make the necessary credit recommendations for students requesting assessment of experiential learning.

Most established programs, as well as those emerging outside the United States, ensure that their faculty are properly trained to assess adults' prior learning, and they conduct periodic reliability studies by having more than one assessor evaluate a person's learning, to ensure the fairness of assessments over time. New faculty also need to be oriented and trained. Colleges show a tendency to invest considerable money in training small cadres of faculty for one- or two-year pilot projects, without extending training to new faculty so that they can understand the process and their respective roles in it as the program expands.

Training programs for faculty most often focus on the nature of adult learners and on how they may be different from more traditional college students. The programs also help faculty begin to think in terms of learning outcomes, standards, and alternative assessment methods. As a rule, few colleges spend much time or money on helping faculty assess learning. It is assumed that, as subject area specialists, they automatically know what students should know and how best to determine whether a particular student has achieved the expected learning. Initial training offered to faculty in many assessment programs is often the only exposure faculty have ever had to good assessment. Thus, training programs offer an exciting opportunity for professional development, reflection, and intellectual inquiry into what is really important in a particular field of study.

Conclusions

Assessing adults' experiential learning provides unique and valuable opportunities to students and faculty alike. It enables students to have their college-level experiential learning recognized and accredited and motivates them to continue pursuing their educational, career, and personal objectives. Similarly, faculty who learn to develop learning outcome statements, set standards, and consider alternative assessment practices will find the assessment process professionally satisfying and enriching to their work as teachers, evaluators, and ultimately, of course, adult learners.

70

References

Chickering, A. *Experience and Learning: An Introduction to Experiential Learning.* New York: Change Magazine Press, 1977.

Cook, M. J. *Developing Learning Outcomes.* Columbia, Md.: Council for the Advancement of Experiential Learning, 1978.

Dewees, P. "Issues in Assessing Occupational and Technical Subjects." In S. Simosko (ed.), *The CAEL Guide to Assessing Prior Learning.* Columbia, Md.: Council for Adult and Experiential Learning, in press.

"Opportunities for Credit." Columbia, Md.: Council for Adult and Experiential Learning, 1986.

Reilly, R. (ed.). *Expert Assessment of Experiential Learning: A CAEL Handbook.* Columbia, Md.: Council for Adult and Experiential Learning, 1977.

Simosko, S. *Earn College Credit for What You Know.* Washington, D.C.: Acropolis Press, 1985.

Susan Simosko was, until September 1987, director of communications of the Council for Adult and Experiential Learning. She recently formed her own company, based in the United Kingdom, where she serves as senior consultant to a national government-funded prior learning assessment project. She continues to work as a workshop facilitator and training adviser in the United States.

*Assessing cumulative learning in the departmental major
requires attention to the purposes of particular evaluation
instruments and to the uses that can be made of results for the
improvement of instruction.*

Assessing the Departmental Major

Bobby Fong

Study in the major field is the centerpiece of the baccalaureate. While educators rightly stress the importance of liberal learning, general competencies, and cocurricular experiences in fully fostering student maturation, the focal point of the college experience remains study in depth, guided most commonly by concentration requirements within an academic department. Given the importance of study in the major, it is surprising how few approaches exist that are appropriate for assessing the cumulative learning that takes place. Any discussion of commercially designed and locally devised instruments, such as the discussion included in this chapter, must consider the purposes and uses of assessment. The very way learning is evaluated is intertwined with a department's conception of its curriculum and expectations for its students.

The usual means of evaluating student achievement in the major are the grades earned in required and elective courses. Unfortunately, writes Chandler (1986), "department major programs characteristically emphasize the number of courses required for a major but usually provide little or no rationale for the major and no compelling statement of the goals of the major" (p. 5). Students must take a specified number of courses from a large list but are provided with no sense of the particular knowledge and skills that a graduate in the field should possess. Beyond

J. H. McMillan (ed.). *Assessing Students' Learning.*
New Directions for Teaching and Learning, no. 34. San Francisco: Jossey-Bass, Summer 1988.

ensuring the quality of individual courses, a department must concern itself with the shape of total learning in the discipline, which may be too dependent on the electives that make up the bulk of work done in the department. The sum of courses taken in a major by a student should add up to something coherent and comprehensive, but that too often is more a matter of hope than of design. For the individual student, few institutions have procedures to determine the degree to which the courses taken actually coalesce into an organized body of knowledge and competencies. For an entire graduating class, there may be no means of guaranteeing that majors share a common core of understanding.

Contexts of Assessments

Objectives, Purposes, and Effects. Methods for assessing cumulative learning have two potential objectives: to gauge individual student achievement, or to measure the performance of majors as a group with regard to common learning. In turn, the results may serve any of three related but distinguishable purposes: to select individuals for postbaccalaureate study or work; to certify basic disciplinary competence of individuals or groups, in order to meet accountability standards of external agencies; or to provide information for program review and improvement. Some assessment methods are particularly well suited to a given objective and purpose; others can serve more than one purpose. It is important to be clear about what is desired in a particular assessment effort and to use methods appropriate to it. Inappropriate methods give an incomplete or even false picture of the teaching and learning in a major program.

It follows that the selection of an assessment method is always embedded in a departmental philosophy of pedagogy and learning, whether enunciated in statements of purpose or implicit in ongoing practice. Selection is based primarily on a method's direct effects: the ways in which its results will be interpreted and used by students, external agencies, the institutional administration, and the department itself. Results may affect enrollment, licensure, funding, hiring, and curriculum requirements and offerings. But a method also has backwash effects in that what and how a department assesses will influence the context, mode, and climate of classroom instruction and learning. The use of a particular approach to evaluation represents a formal declaration by a department about the materials it believes important for students to know, abilities it expects students to demonstrate, and practices it wants to encourage among instructors. Also, what is omitted from an assessment has consequences. Frederiksen (1984) notes, "If educational tests fail to represent the spectrum of knowledge and skills that ought to be taught, they may introduce bias against teaching important skills that are not measured" (p. 193). Choosing or devising an approach to evaluate cumulative achievement in the major demands attention to the objectives, purposes, and effects of the approach.

Expectations and Faculty Culture. Assessing a major program engages a faculty in the process of forging agreement on what the major means. Politically, this is where attempts to assess the major flounder. An electives-based curriculum in the major can maximize the freedom of faculty to move between the specializations of scholarship and the demands of the classroom. One teaches from the results of one's research. It also, however, encourages the proliferation of courses that constitute narrower and narrower slices of a discipline. Depth of study is achieved at the expense of breadth, and since students have only a limited number of courses to take in the major, expertise is achieved at the expense of comprehensiveness. The situation is exacerbated by current developments in fields where the notion of "canons," or a tradition of established authorities and readings, is being challenged. The appropriateness of a text depends on audience, culture, and pedagogical aim. The very presumption that there can be an identifiable core of necessary knowledge for a major becomes the point of dispute. I do not impugn the importance of research specialization or the critique of canons, for both represent the means to more sophisticated understanding of fields of knowledge. At the same time, if the major is to remain a viable basis of organizing knowledge for pedagogical purposes, then departmental faculty must engage in discussing the structure and function of that organization. The major is a pedagogical schema for the transmission of knowledge and skills. That is why a department requires a certain number of courses in the major, a critical mass of achievement. As a pedagogical schema, the major represents what the members of the department believe to be the necessary and sufficient attainments of a baccalaureate graduate in the discipline.

I make this point at length because without a determination to define the rationale and content of the major, assessment cannot proceed. Validity in assessment depends on the correspondence between what is tested and the body of knowledge and skills deemed important to be assessed. If faculty are not able to enunciate what they seek in a graduate in the major, they will not be in a good position to determine the appropriateness of an instrument, since they cannot specify what they seek to measure.

The goals of the major can be described in a number of ways—a designation of content, an enumeration of proficiencies, a declaration that the culminating work of a student be certifiable by acknowledged experts—but whether it is to measure individual student learning or the learning of an entire cohort, assessment presumes that a department will enunciate the meaning of the major. The agreement may be local rather than national, a reflection of the particular priorities and expertise of the individual department, and it will likely change over time. But assessment to measure student achievement needs a clear declaration of what faculty expect students to achieve.

A disciplinary field is defined by a common vocabulary of discourse, common concerns, and a common body of knowledge and techniques. Like natives of a culture, disciplinary faculty normally do not think about how they are distinguishable from the foreigners seeking to learn the folkways. As conveyers of the academic culture of the major, however, faculty need to give thought to exactly this matter, and departmental assessments of the major become occasions for such consideration. Chandler (1986) writes, "As I recall my own teaching career, I believe that some of the most valuable investment of my time was in the long hours that my colleagues and I spent designing questions and exercises for final examinations in the introductory course and for the comprehensive departmental examination. . . . Working together on those examinations compelled us to review the purposes and goals of particular courses and consider the rationale of the overall structure of the departmental curriculum. Furthermore, those conversations were extremely valuable for young members of the department who were still making the transition from graduate student to full-time teacher" (pp. 6-7).

Assessment of the major thus entails far more than the choice of an appropriate method. It requires consideration of objective, purpose, and effects, and it is preceded and continually sustained by recurrent faculty discussion of the rationale and content of the major. The major and its assessment are expressions of the culture of the discipline, represented and maintained by the faculty. These contexts must be kept in mind if the ensuing discussion of particular assessment approaches is to have any connection with the essential contribution of assessment: the yielding of information to support and improve teaching and learning.

Commercially Designed Examinations

Pros and Cons. Commercially available examinations have the advantage of being field-tested. They also permit the scores of individuals to be compared against national norms. The costs of these tests are high, typically above $30 per exam; but, being scored by machine, they do not make additional demands on faculty. Finally, the use of standardized examinations for licensure, certification, and admission to graduate study accords them authority among faculty, since the success or failure of majors on such instruments reflects directly on preparation received in the major program.

There are also a number of drawbacks to commercially available assessment devices. National examinations, by definition, do not respond to local emphases. A commercial test may not reflect what a particular department is trying to do. Then there is the matter of the multiple-choice format. Objective tests are a superior means of sampling knowledge and comprehension, because the number of questions posed in a given time can be greater than might be possible in essay formats. At the same time, as Frederiksen (1984), Elton (1982), and Rowntree (1977) have argued, such a format is ill suited to the examination of such higher-order skills as analysis, synthesis, and evaluation, for which students should respond to open-ended situations that call on a range of appropriate strategies. Moreover, the associated skill of being able to express oneself in expository prose is given short shrift.

Beyond content and format limitations, there is a difficulty in using the results of such examinations. Scores can be reported for individuals and groups, and certain exams can break performance down to subject subscores. Nevertheless, without item analyses, which cannot be made available without retiring the questions in that edition of the test, it is difficult to use the information to improve program instruction. Furthermore, most commercially prepared achievement tests are not designed to compare a student's performance to an absolute standard of knowledge or skill, but to the performance of others. Such selection-referenced tests are intended to maximize individual differences for purposes of comparison, in contrast to criterion-referenced tests, which seek to determine how much of a body of knowledge one knows, or how skillful one is, according to some preset standard. Harris (1986) cautions, "The selection test approach works well when the purpose is to spread individuals over a continuum. But it is awkward, to say the least, when the purpose is to certify a level of competence" (p. 16).

A final concern with the use of commercial instruments is the discontinuity between faculty control over instruction and faculty participation in assessment. If scoring is done by machine, and if results are only minimally useful as an aid to improving instruction, then the numbers generated by such tests may serve the purposes of external accountability or selection for postbaccalaureate activity without ever involving faculty in questions of curriculum and learning.

Current Instruments. Preprofessional majors such as nursing and education have licensure and certification processes that include commercially prepared examinations. The cutoff point for passing is set by state or professional bodies, and while faculty may have some influence on content and standards, the assessment instruments are beyond the control of any particular local department. The immediate object and purpose is to evaluate individuals for postbaccalaureate employment, but pass rates of graduating classes provide a measure of an institution's performance in teaching the necessary knowledge and skills. The effect has been to encourage standardized curricular offerings.

The situation is different for the liberal arts and the sciences, where a major does not presume a particular vocational outcome. Here, curricular offerings differ from institution to institution, and responsibility rests on local faculty to assess for learning, using instruments appropriate to departmental emphases. Some departments have chosen to require that all prospective graduates take the GRE area examinations in the appropriate disciplines. These tests, however, were designed to show students' command of curricula commonly offered to prepare undergraduates for graduate study. There is a problem with validity in the use of tests constructed to predict success in graduate study as measures of learning by all students in a major. The selection-referenced basis of the test may not be a good indicator of basic competence in the field. Moreover, since most liberal arts graduates do not go on to postbaccalaureate study in their disciplines, curricula designed to propagate graduate study may serve most majors badly.

Both the College-Level Examination Program (CLEP) subject examinations and the ACT Proficiency Examination Program (PEP) traditionally have been used to assess proficiency for the purpose of awarding college credit in lieu of the student's taking a course. Interest has developed, however, in using such exams for outcomes assessment after the student has taken the appropriate course (examples are projects discussed in "College-Level Examination Program at 20 . . . , 1987). While this may be a legitimate use of the tests to measure learning within a course, "they are not designed to reflect the comprehensive proficiency expected of a graduating senior in a major field" (Harris, 1986, p. 22). An alternative—to administer the entire battery of such tests in a given discipline—would be time-consuming and expensive.

New Developments. Between course-specific examinations and tests to select candidates for graduate study, there is a gap that may be filled by the proposed major field achievement tests of the Educational Testing Service (ETS). The GRE area examinations are being revised to become measures of cumulative learning in the major. They will be offered in one- and two-hour formats. The shorter form will yield aggregate information on the group of test takers at a particular administration; the longer one will give individual scores as well. Subscore breakdowns will be extensive enough to indicate strengths and weaknesses in particular subjects, so as to aid in program improvement. Comparative norms will be available, both nationally and by institutional groupings selected by individual departments as peer institutions. The tests will become available in September of this year.

In addition, two other ETS pilot projects may have long-term benefits for assessing the major. The Item-Banking Workshop will be a series of seminars to train faculty in writing test questions for end-of-course assessment in specific disciplines. The items will be edited and classified by test development staff and then pooled in a computer bank, from which tests can be constructed by faculty for local use. If a battery of subjects in a discipline can eventually be represented in the bank, faculty will be able to construct local comprehensives with items already reviewed by professional staff. The Benchmark Performance Technique is another ETS project, which will have faculty prepare end-of-course assessments in specific disciplines, using non–multiple-choice formats. Assessment of quality will involve the development of benchmark criteria for competence. An example of this approach would be the specimen essays in writing evaluations that embody standards of excellence, adequacy, and failure. Over the long term, development of benchmark performance standards should help faculty develop criteria for judging senior projects and other demonstrations of higher learning that exceed the limits of multiple-choice tests.

Locally Devised Approaches

Pros and Cons. Currently, no commercial instrument is wholly appropriate for assessing the cumulative learning of all students in the major, and results from available commercial tests should be supplemented by existing measures, such as grades, and by locally devised instruments. Characteristically, the most successful and enduring local approaches have tended to eschew the multiple-choice format in favor of processes whereby the student can demonstrate ability to structure the paths to a solution, not simply select an answer from a list of possibilities. There are wrong answers and interesting wrong answers. The path by which a student assays a problem can be as revealing of mastery of the discipline as the particular answer obtained. Moreover, the emphasis in using such approaches as senior projects or comprehensives shifts from probing for gaps in learning (as in multiple-choice examinations) to providing a range of options from which students choose topics or questions that exhibit their interests and learning to best advantage. Primary attention is focused on what students do know and can do.

For this chapter, I will describe five assessment methods: theses and projects, orals, comprehensives, portfolios, and external examiners. These methods have been used singly and in various combinations at particular institutions, but a common characteristic of all five is the centrality of faculty in planning, administering, and evaluating them and their results. Controlled by local faculty, these methods remain sensitive to local educational missions and interests. Furthermore, faculty are involved in both instruction and assessment, rather than having these efforts separated by use of a method external to the duties of the department. Feedback regarding student performance tends to be more immediate, and students' successes as well as their failures are more readily owned by faculty, since performance has been tested by an instrument of the department's own devising.

However, involvement in assessment also represents an additional demand on instructors' time and energy. The determination to do assessment bespeaks a concern to demonstrate the quality of teaching and learning, but the temptation exists to avoid the requisite demand on faculty resources, which may already be stretched thin. Yet easing the faculty role in assessment means attenuating the usefulness of the process for understanding and aiding program improvement. If assessment is to be done well, faculty must be at the center of the effort.

One final problem with locally controlled efforts is that they may not give results that are readily comparable across institutions. There must be some provision for gaining perspective on how the standards and expectations of the department compare against those of peer institutions; otherwise, a department's own view of its educational effectiveness may remain skewed and provincial. At the same time, the difficulties of coming up with easily comparable results may not be altogether undesirable: Institutions are justifiably leery of having student scores on an instrument reported without consideration for educational mission, student preparation and interests, and program emphases. An open-admissions state university may not post scores that are as high as those of a selective, private liberal arts college, but it would be grossly unfair to assume that the disparity necessarily results from differences in instructional effectiveness.

Theses and Projects. In-depth study may culminate in the opportunity for independent study as a capstone experience. Green (1987), writing of Bradford College, reports that all majors must complete a senior project. "The student is asked to pose a significant question and, with the aid of a faculty advisor, work that question through to a solution and produce a final project in the form of a research paper, manuscript, portfolio, exhibit, or performance. This task demands that the student apply and demonstrate the skills and knowledge acquired over four years. It serves also as evidence of the student's passage to the stage of independent learner and producer."

Theses and projects have been widely required of candidates for honors degrees, and less frequently demanded of all majors in a department. The approach encourages the individual student to pursue his or her own interests and exhibit a personal synthesis of a field. Since each project is unique, this approach succeeds less well at revealing common learning for all majors or inspiring comparable products. Indeed, since a project is usually an investigation of a narrow aspect of the discipline, the results may show little evidence even of the individual's comprehensive learning.

Another concern is whether independent work is a suitable task for students not able or committed to do honors-level work. The prospect that completing a thesis or project, drawn out over most of the senior year, may determine whether one graduates can be fearsome for less accomplished students and frustrating to their advisors. Reed College, which also requires senior theses and projects, administers junior qualifying examinations, consisting of a research paper, an essay exam, a group of problems, an oral, or another activity, which a student must pass before proceeding to the thesis.

A final concern has to do with evaluation. Unless a project is assessed by faculty other than the adviser, it remains a species of course work, not an exercise in mastery that can be recognized by authorities not previously involved in the activity; both Reed and Bradford require that projects and theses be evaluated by other faculty.

Orals. In addition to the thesis, Reed requires a two-hour oral examination by a board consisting of the project advisor, representatives from the same academic division, and at least one faculty member from outside the division. The exam includes a presentation of the thesis or project and an extended question-and-answer session that relates the work to the larger context of the examinee's studies. Departmental faculty are especially interested in students' ability to present their disciplines to people outside their fields.

King College in Tennessee uses visiting scholars and knowledgeable members of the community to administer half-hour oral interviews to honors candidates in the major. An ancillary benefit of such encounters has been the offer of jobs or fellowships for graduate study. A current Association of American Colleges (AAC) project, "Assessing Learning in Academic Majors Using External Faculty Examiners," includes participating institutions experimenting with oral examinations by having faculty interview groups of students. One possible strategy is to present each group with a problem or set of topics ahead of time and allow students to fashion a presentation, to be followed by questions. The assumption is that free-ranging discussion between students and faculty can be a valuable indicator of students' mastery of the discourse and methods of a field. In addition, students have some control over the direction of discussion and can use the situation to exhibit strengths. Specific knowledge can only be sampled, of course, and the open-endedness of discussion may preclude any probing for comprehensive knowledge. For the same reason, it would be difficult to use orals alone to test for common learning across the group. There is also the problem that less voluble or slower-witted students may suffer in comparison to others. Nevertheless, the use of oral presentations, interviews, and examinations has proved a useful way to assess learning, particularly when these techniques are paired with projects or theses that provide initial points of focus.

Comprehensives. The particular need to assess for common learning, in addition to examining the individualized learning exhibited by projects, theses, and orals, suggests the use of comprehensive examinations. The posing of a common set of questions or problems to the entire class of prospective graduates in a major both establishes expectations of essential learning and probes to see if such learning has been achieved. At the same time, offering some range of choice among the questions allows students to pursue lines of inquiry that reflect the emphases of their individual elective programs. The British university comprehensive examination system, where students from different colleges sit for a common set of disciplinary exams, has long been a means of maintaining program quality and comparability across departments.

There is also the backwash of such exams on programs and curricula. Historically, comprehensive examinations were designed to evaluate student learning; but, as Resnick and Goulden (1987) have noted, "they had the auxiliary effect of directing attention to the departmental curriculum, and the way the student ha[d] been prepared. Many institutions introduced reading lists, tutorials, senior seminars, and other restructurings of the undergraduate program that were designed to aid the student's performance" (p. 6).

Essential to the process, however, is the commitment of the departmental faculty. Advising a senior project or thesis is an extension of independent study arrangements, with which most faculty are comfortable. Administering oral examinations demands more scheduling and preparation, but the work of evaluating the performance is done during the oral. By contrast, written comprehensives demand that faculty meet each year to create the examination and, after the administration, to read and grade the papers. It is a substantial investment of time, and the process of agreeing to questions and norming marks can be stressful. There must be the conviction that the benefits to student learning (mainly in the preparation for comps) and to enhanced program coherence will repay the labor.

Portfolios. For students, the value of projects, theses, orals, and comprehensives lies primarily in their preparation and research. Judgments of such work usually come toward the end of matriculation, and unless a student fails and must repeat the work, the marks and comments rendered by reviewers simply certify the performance, rather than correcting and suggesting with an eye to further learning in the program. By contrast, the value of a portfolio approach, in which students are required over several years to assemble pieces of work attesting to their mastery, is that there can be mechanisms built in for continuous assessment, while students can still benefit from faculty suggestions.

At Alverno College, the Arts and Humanities division has an arrangement whereby the student, with the assistance of a departmental adviser, begins assembling a portfolio from the time he or she begins study in an area of concentration. Over two or three years, the student selects exemplary papers (including those where disciplinary knowledge and skills have been brought to bear on courses outside the field), speech notes, videotapes, and other records of performances that attest to achievement in the subject. At the end of the junior year, the student writes an analytical essay remarking on how the portfolio represents certain disciplinary emphases and approaches, relation to other areas of study, and areas of weakness to be remedied. A panel of faculty, including one faculty member from outside the division, reviews the essay and portfolio and, in a one-hour oral interview, probes for further learning and makes recommendations for additional study in the field.

The great advantage of this arrangement is that the student can still benefit from faculty feedback. Rather than offering a summary judgment, this process allows for continuous assessment from the advisor and the panel. Furthermore, the products for assessment are actually those produced in the course of study, not specimens generated solely to exhibit summative learning. It should be possible to chart growth as well as achievement. Like senior projects and theses, however, portfolios shed more light on individual learning than on common learning across a group. The process also calls for a good deal of coordination and scheduling, and it relies heavily on the advisor-student relationship. The advisor becomes the principal tutor. (One positive effect may be to rejuvenate a task that in many institutions consists only of signing a schedule card once a term.)

External Examiners. This means of assessment is actually a component to be used in conjunction with one or more of the first four. O'Neill (1983) writes, "There is a conflict of interest in the way in which American colleges and universities certify instruction. . . . Faculty members not only teach but in effect guarantee, first, that their teaching meets established standards in both content and quality and, second, that students have learned what faculty have taught. There is no external mechanism to verify the integrity of the baccalaureate degree" (p. 71).

One answer is to invite faculty from other institutions and knowledgeable outsiders to serve as panelists or reviewers for projects, orals, comprehensives, or portfolios. External examiners offer a way to certify learning, without being open to the charge of conflict of interest, since they can assess student achievement without having departmental or institutional stakes in the outcome. This arrangement, of course, is an integral part of the British comprehensive system.

The best-known example of an ongoing American external-examiner arrangement is at Swarthmore College. There, the designation of honors depends solely on performance in the senior year on a series of comprehensive examinations and oral interviews prepared and graded by external faculty examiners. Students undertake a series of seminars beginning in the junior year, and the terminal examinations are on the seminar topics, not on an entire discipline. Nevertheless, the coverage afforded by the entire series of examinations is substantial.

The AAC project, already mentioned, is based on the Swarthmore model. It experiments with the use of written comprehensives, or other exercises, and oral examinations administered by outside examiners. Eighteen institutions have been clustered in groups of three, according to characteristics of region, institutional size, and similarity of academic program offerings. Each cluster has designated three majors that its institutions will examine in common. Beginning this year, fifteen students graduating in a given major will be examined by faculty in that discipline from the other two institutions of the cluster. Results will be provided to students, and visiting examiners will report to the department and to the institutional officers to help them assess how the objectives of the major are being met.

The use of visiting examiners represents a means of establishing external accountability. It may also lead to some comparability between departmental programs, if sister institutions that exchange examiners also agree to use the same comprehensive examinations or other exercises. The logistics of scheduling, costs for travel, and remuneration are causes for concern, however. In the British system, there now exists a tradition that serving as an examiner is a part of a tutor's normal duties and that remuneration is nominal. This is not the case in America. Still, Swarthmore and other institutions that have used external examiners (see Fong, 1987) find that faculty and industry professionals are willing to serve at rates far below their usual fees, because of the opportunity to learn about other programs and enhance their own companies and departments. It represents an extension of service to the profession and the community, and it reflects a desire to work with peers across institutional boundaries to facilitate the education of the next generation of professionals and academics.

Conclusion

Assessing a major is no simple matter of choosing or devising a method. Indeed, as the preceding discussion suggests, there is no one test or approach that is sufficient by itself to serve all the objectives and purposes of assessment. A strong case can be made for a multidimensional strategy, in which instruments are complementary, the combination depending on the priorities of local faculty to shape curricula to meet goals for students. Assessment cannot be justified as an end in itself; it will be a sterile exercise unless its results contribute to the support and improvement of teaching and learning.

References

Chandler, J. W. "The College Perspective on Assessment." Paper presented at an invitational conference sponsored by the Educational Testing Service, New York City, October 25, 1986.

"College-Level Examination Program at 20: Leading the Way in Higher Education Assessment." *The College Board News*, 1987, *15* (3), 4.

Elton, L. "Assessment for Learning." In D. Bligh (ed.), *Professionalism and Flexibility in Learning*. Surrey, England: Society for Research in Higher Education, 1982.

Fong, B. "The External Examiner Approach to Assessment." Paper commissioned for the Second National Conference on Assessment in Higher Education, sponsored by the American Association for Higher Education, Denver, Colo., June 14–17, 1987.

Frederiksen, N. "The Real Test Bias: Influences of Testing on Teaching and Learning." *American Psychologist*, 1984, *39* (3), 193–202.

Green, J. "Assessment at Bradford College." Unpublished memorandum, Bradford College, 1987.

Harris, J. "Assessing Outcomes in Higher Education." In C. Adelman (ed.), *Assessment in American Higher Education*. Washington, D.C.: U.S. Department of Education, 1986.

O'Neill, J. P. "Examinations and Quality Control." In J. R. Warren (ed.), *Meeting the New Demands for Standards*. New Directions for Higher Education, no. 43. San Francisco: Jossey-Bass, 1983.

Resnick, D. P., and Goulden, M. "Assessment, Curriculum and Expansion in American Higher Education: A Historical Perspective." Paper presented at the Second National Conference on Assessment in Higher Education, sponsored by the American Association for Higher Education, Denver, Colo., June 14–17, 1987.

Rowntree, D. *Assessing Students: How Shall We Know Them?* London: Harper & Row, 1977.

Bobby Fong is associate professor of English at Berea College, Berea, Kentucky. During 1986–87, he was a national fellow with the Association of American Colleges, Washington, D.C., where he served as assistant director for the project "Assessing Learning in Academic Majors Using External Faculty Examiners," underwritten by the Fund for the Improvement of Postsecondary Education.

*Grades should be a way for teachers and students to
communicate about student performance. Using grades to rank
and sort is detrimental to learning and to the development of
a stimulating and supportive academic climate.*

Grading Students

Howard R. Pollio, W. Lee Humphreys

Grading outstrips both intercollegiate athletics and intramural sports as
the most frequently played game on the college campus. It takes place in
all seasons, and everyone gets to play one position or another. As in
other sports, the grading game yields a plethora of statistics, around
which has developed a distinct and mystical numerology. A conservative
estimate suggests that with roughly 12 million students enrolled in two-
and four-year institutions of higher education in the United States, and
with each student taking three or four courses per term, between 72 million and 96 million final course grades are assigned each year. There is
no telling how many individual grades are given for specific assignments,
tests, papers, lab reports, projects, public performances, class participation, and even attendance. Once given, these grades generally are blended
into a single number called the grade point average (GPA), which is
taken to the second decimal or beyond. We all are aware that very important decisions that profoundly shape the future lives of students may be
made on the basis of the GPA.

Grades, grading, and the uses made of them strongly affect the
academic climate within which teaching and learning take place. With
the exception of very few institutions, grades and the grading game are
basic facts of academic life for professors and students, and they influence
in many and varied ways important interactions between teachers and
learners. We want to argue that we should do everything possible to

J. H. McMillan (ed.). *Assessing Students' Learning.*
New Directions for Teaching and Learning, no. 34. San Francisco: Jossey-Bass, Summer 1988.

ensure that grades and grading enrich the academic setting, facilitate fruitful interactions between instructors and students, and serve to augment rather than impede the course of college learning. We can begin by reflecting on some things everyone "knows" about college grades, to see if new implications may be drawn from these familiar facts.

Common Knowledge About Grades

There is nothing esoteric about the following five facts; they are simply common knowledge that students, instructors, and administrators share about grades. Even though they are known, we may not understand all they imply.

Different instructors produce grades in different ways. As college professors, we have received and given grades. From both perspectives, we know that some instructors grade against an absolute standard and measure student products against this norm, others allocate grades on some sort of curve that ranks each student in relation to his or her peers, and still other instructors stress the amount of growth or development a student demonstrates (that is, they grade the degree to which potential has been developed or realized). Using any of these methods, it is always possible to nuance grading still further by taking account of such factors as class cuts, tardiness, absence due to illness, personal problems, and so on.

The meaning of any grade assigned to a student depends in part on the priorities of the individual instructor who gives it. Grades are determined by the values of individual instructors who teach individual disciplines, and these values give grades their specific operational form. How we grade reveals what we value. Most of us who give grades find that as the grade leaves our hands, and certainly as it leaves our classroom in the form of a final grade report, all indications of the unique procedures and values underlying it are stripped from the notation. A single letter on a transcript bears no trace of the way in which that grade was produced nor of the instructor's procedures, priorities, and values. An A from one professor is not the same as an A from a second professor.

The quality, nature, and number of classroom tests vary. Instructors may take account of many things when they assign grades, but tests usually have a central position. It is no secret that the quality, number, and nature of classroom tests vary from class to class, discipline to discipline, and college to college. Some instructors let it all ride on a final exam, some give a midterm and a final, and some use frequent quizzes. Some instructors prefer essays, while others prefer "objective" tests, generally of the multiple-choice variety. Some essay tests tap little more than simple recall, asking only that the student give information in sentences and paragraphs. Some essay questions seem well designed and focused;

others are so vague as to invite the strategic nonsense some students become adept at producing. Multiple-choice tests normally ask for recognition of items rather than recollection, and studies indicate that most of them tap little more than recognition (Milton, 1982). Indeed, it takes thought and practice to produce multiple-choice items that involve higher orders of critical and creative thinking. Most faculty have had little training in constructing such test items, and too few discuss classroom testing with colleagues, even though there is ample evidence, both long-standing (Class, 1935; Balch, 1964; Hakstian, 1971) and of more recent origin (Milton, 1982; Eison, Pollio, and Cunningham, in press), to indicate that what and how we test is a powerful force in shaping what and how students learn. Certainly what is tested and how it is tested is rarely apparent in a grade notation, especially outside the immediate classroom context. The testing procedure vanishes when the grade is buried in the transcript and in the GPA.

Cheating goes on in college classrooms. Attempts to prevent cheating are many, and some are so elaborate as to distort the context for teaching and learning. Yet cheating goes on anyway. A recent national survey of attitudes toward grades and grading (Milton, Pollio, and Eison, 1986) indicates that over one-half of students surveyed reported having cheated to improve a grade. When faculty, parents, and business groups were asked the same question, the values were 36 percent, 34 percent, and 42 percent, respectively. The present generation of students does not have a monopoly on cheating, even if their elders seem a bit less guilty. Students recognize in this perverse way that grades are powerful and valuable tokens.

The pedagogical practices of many faculty members reinforce the message that grades are important, and parents as well as others add their weight to this view. Questionnaire results reveal that grades are valued by students, their parents, and others as symbols of much more than test results or academic attainment. Pollio, Humphreys, and Milton (1987) found that these groups believe that grades reflect such personal traits as psychological adjustment, the ability to work in a system, intelligence, self-discipline, and personal motivation. If these connotations are not enough to indicate how significant grades are to all players in the grading game, it is also clear that important extracollegiate decisions are made on the basis of grades. A person's GPA can open or close doors of opportunity that may determine the course of his or her professional and personal life. Even such crucial issues as the cost of a student's auto insurance is influenced by the GPA. It's little wonder that students are tempted to cheat.

Grading stakes are high for faculty and students alike. Little can rival the grading game as a wedge in relationships between instructors and students. No other factor is as powerful either in leading students to subvert the academic process in leading faculty to behave in an autocratic or adversarial way. There may be areas where faculty and students perceive certain actions differently with regard to whether they constitute cheating (for example, collaboration; see Barnett and Dalton, 1981), but there are others where all agree on what constitutes cheating, and such activities are not uncommon in the classroom.

Some students are interested in making grades but not in learning. With stakes so high, for some students the grading game has taken on a life of its own, distinct and separate from learning. On the basis of the way in which students answered a questionnaire designed to determine orientation toward both learning and grades, researchers have come to classify students as learning oriented, grade oriented, or some combination of the two (Milton, 1982; Milton, Pollio, and Eison, 1986; Eison, Pollio, and Milton, 1986; Eison, Pollio, and Cunningham, in press). In practice, four different groups of students are defined by the combination of being high or low on both grade and learning orientations. Perhaps the single most revealing way to spot a grade-oriented student in the classroom is to notice who asks the dreaded question "Will that be on the exam?" A negative answer invariably leads to an immediate and irrevocable loss of the student's interest, no matter how brilliant the instructor's presentation.

Characterizing someone as a high- or low-grade or learning-oriented student has been shown to relate to the ways in which that student performs in class and to what he or she values about this experience. For example, Eison, Pollio, and Cunningham (in press) found that students with a high grade orientation prefer multiple-choice exams more than students with a learning orientation do; they state that they usually find such tests easier to take or that they have done better on them in the past. Not one grade-oriented student selecting a multiple-choice test felt it fostered better or more significant learning. In contrast, students with a stronger orientation toward learning than toward grades indicated greater preference for essay tests, and while they gave similar reasons for their choice of test format, some suggested they felt essay tests better reflected their abilities and that preparing for such tests facilitated learning.

In another study designed to determine what students did and thought about during lectures (Pollio, 1984), grade-oriented students were found to be off target more than learning-oriented students were. Even when grade-oriented students were perceived by a trained observer to be on target in terms of what they were doing, they were off target in their self-reports of what they were paying attention to a significant percent of the time. The grading game is so intense that for some students attaining a good grade stands in direct competition with the cardinal purpose of higher education: to learn all you can, whether the information will be tested or not.

College professors got better grades than anyone else. While for a number of students grades themselves are significant enough to detract from learning, most instructors know that students do not really value grades as highly as they themselves do. This may be largely because college professors tend on the whole to have been winners in the grading game. Results of a national survey (Milton, Pollio, and Eison, 1986) revealed that 61 percent of 854 current faculty members reported having received "mostly A's" in college. Comparable values were 23 percent for 4,365 current students, 25 percent for 362 business recruiters, and 32 percent for 584 parents. We will describe some of the specific ways in which faculty differ from students and others in their perceptions of grades; that such perceptions vary comes as no surprise. We have all known students who are driven by grades and who nevertheless perceive grades as tokens of little worth in themselves or in relation to learning, but of immense value in the larger struggle for position and privilege—a struggle in which colleges and universities serve more and more as institutions for sorting, ranking, and selecting people.

These brief reflections on things everybody knows about grades suggest above all else that they are context-determined phenomena. The meaning of a grade depends on the factors that determine the specific climate of the class in which it is assigned. Primary among these factors are the priorities and procedures that instructors use in assigning grades, as well as the nature and quality of tests and other assignments on which the grade is based. There also seem to be marked differences in the meaning grades have for professors and students, with professors overvaluing their own symbols. Grades may appear to be context-determined symbols for communication between teachers and students, but on transcripts and in the GPA they have taken on a weight and a life of their own, quite distinct from and even in competition with their uses in teaching and learning. This state of affairs has led some students and instructors into practices that are inimical to the academic climate of cooperation and mutual trust that facilitates genuine learning. Cheating becomes commonplace, and learning takes second place to grading.

Uncommon Knowledge About Grades

A more effective use of grades in teaching and learning can be approached by considering additional information about grades, information that may not be very well known.

Grades did not always have the five major categories A through F. In the history of higher education, letter grades are relative latecomers, especially in the form we know them today. In 1783 the first grades in this country were given at Yale. Four categories—Optime, Second Optime, Inferiors, and Pejores—were used to describe the totality of a student's year. One suspects that deportment and decorum were as formative as academic attainment in shaping the grade. It was not until a century later that the first letter grade—a B—was given at Yale. Over the next century, there were marked swings in the number of units that defined the various grading scales employed (see Milton, Pollio, and Eison, 1986). These ranged, for example, from two units (Pass/Fail or Pass/No Credit) in the sixties and early seventies of this century to a system with five to thirteen units (A through F, often with pluses and minuses) to one with one hundred to four hundred units (percentages, or the 0.00-4.00 scale used by some law schools).

Grades were not always as pervasive a part of academic life as they are now and in the form we give them today. Even more interesting, regular swings in the number and nature of grading systems seem to correspond to larger swings in societal concern for standards, accountability, and the ranking of people on the one hand, and individual growth and group consensus and support on the other. Grading systems reflect a contrast—between competitive ranking and cooperative support—that pervades our society more generally. Through the grading of students and the use made or allowed to be made of grades, higher education has responded to and been shaped by larger societal and historical trends. Grades, which serve as a mode of communication in higher education, have become reified (above all in the GPA) and are used to sort and rank people for jobs, professions, and often the advanced training needed to enter them. Grades often skew the academic climate, and the manner in which the grading game has come to have a life of its own can be traced to these latter uses of grades.

Do we really need so many units in our grading systems if we use grades to communicate with students about their mastery of material and skills in specific courses? Some instructors may be comfortable employing more categories (A through F, complete with pluses and minuses); others may find Honors, Certified, and Not Certified enough. Instructors should never be required to use scales more finely calibrated than their powers or desires to discriminate among students. Our tests should be designed to tap significant information and permit students to demonstrate knowledge of important material and skills. We will not need to tap trivia, or to test obscurities buried in footnotes, if we avoid the trap of ranking all our students and making the minute discriminations required to assign positions on some multiunit scale. We do not argue here for a standard number of units; this decision should be made by the individual instructor. What we do suggest is that the symbols used to communicate between teacher and student not exceed the instructor's power and need to discriminate. Our primary purpose is not to rank, but to determine what students have learned and to help them improve if we feel they have not learned well enough.

SATs and GPAs are related in a very odd way. Milton, Pollio, and Eison (1986) studied the rise and fall of SAT scores and GPAs from 1950 to 1980. The findings were striking: When one goes up, the other goes down. There may be some debate about just what the SAT (or the ACT) measures, but whatever it is, when student performance on the SAT goes down, GPAs have gone up, and when student performance on the SAT has gone up, GPAs have gone down. By SAT standards, better students at one historical moment are being graded more stringently than weaker students at another historical moment. Thus, the relationship between what the SAT measures and GPAs is not what is usually assumed to be the case. Moreover, the value of the grades that make up a student's GPA is not standard across historical periods. Once again it is apparent that grades are meaningful only in the immediate context in which they are given; grades are not an unequivocal set of symbols that bear absolute meanings when stripped of contextual factors. It also appears that grade contexts are shaped not only by the values and practices of individual instructors and students but also by qualities of the larger historical era in which grades are given.

Faculty, students, parents, and business people do not agree on what grades "really" mean. In their national survey of attitudes toward grades, Milton, Pollio, and Eison (1986) designed several questions to determine what grades meant to students, faculty, parents, and potential employers. While there were areas of agreement across groups, there were also some striking areas of disagreement. For example, when asked how long they thought the difference between an A and a C would last, 53 percent of faculty members felt it would last from two to five years or longer; only 14 percent of students felt this way. Of the students, however, 45 percent felt any difference between an A and a C was simply nonexistent or would last at most for three months; only 14 percent of faculty members agreed with this opinion. The duration of whatever a grade measures is simply not apparent to many students, even when they regard the grade as an important token.

Parents' and business respondents' opinions about grades also differed from those of students and faculty. In regard to how long the differences between an A and a C would last, 34 percent of parents and only 19 percent of business respondents felt that such differences were nonexistent or would last less than three months. When we look at the other end of the scale and compare values for the view that A–C differences last two to four years or longer, results revealed that 33 percent of parents and 32 percent of business respondents reported this as their belief. These additional results suggest that to those who received good grades in their own student days—college instuctors—grades appear to convey significant and long-lasting information about the abilities of the students to whom they are assigned. Parents and business respondents are somewhat more sanguine than current students about grades, but they also tend to view grades as less significant than college professors do. Whatever else this may suggest, it indicates all too often that faculty and students are giving and receiving symbols about whose significance they disagree markedly. The same difference in perception also applies to the two major users of the symbols: business people and parents.

The older generation—faculty, parents, and business recruiters—did agree on one issue: their belief that grades predict future success. For these three groups, 37 percent, 39 percent, and 35 percent checked the categories of "high" or "very high" in describing their views of the relationship between college grades and future success in life. The comparable value for students was 25 percent, again suggesting that students see much less value in grades than others do.

We have argued that grades should be viewed as addressed essentially to students within the specific context of an individual classroom and course—indeed, the results of the national grade survey found that faculty and students agree this should be the primary use of grades—but all groups also recognize that grades are addressed to and used by others. It is therefore striking that while 80 percent of business recruiters look at the GPA, over 70 percent of companies that have minimum cutoff scores use 2.75 (or less) as their value. Given the ambiguities that surround the GPA, such a low cutoff seems wise. Only 11 percent of business recruiters report that their companies have conducted any studies evaluating the predictive value of grades. It almost appears as if the use of the GPA in decisions made by business recruiters reflects a ritualistic legacy, a homage to semisacred symbols whose import is lost in ambiguity. While 38 percent of business recruiters say grades are of "great" importance for initial hiring, only 16 percent say grades determine initial salary or selection for special training programs, and only 2 percent consider grades of "great" importance for subsequent promotions.

To link this result with selection procedures used to admit students to graduate school, faculty and business recruiters were asked to rank-order several criteria for selecting graduate students or employees. Although both faculty and recruiters viewed grades in major courses as one major criterion for selection, the remaining criteria that both groups considered of great significance were different. Graduate-selection faculty deemed the following items crucial: number of difficult courses completed, breadth of courses taken, scores on standardized tests, and samples of student writing. For business, the following items were considered most important: nature of noncollege jobs held, student personality, and participation in extracurricular activities. It seems clear that business recruiters consider a lot of nonacademic factors in selecting employees.

There is not much correlation between grades and future success in life. Responses on the degree to which grades are believed predict future success were different for student and faculty groups. Students saw grades as having little predictive potential for future success (21 percent saw them as of little or no use, and 25 percent saw them as highly useful), while faculty saw them as having good predictive potential (only 10 percent saw them as having no use, and 37 percent saw them as highly useful). Results of a host of correlational analyses reveal that students are closer to the mark than their "markers" are. At least four major reviews (Hoyt, 1965; Nelson, 1975; Cohen, 1984; Baird, 1985) point to the same conclusion: The data do not support the common faculty view, and this is bound to be surprising to most faculty members. A basic result yielded by these surveys—and these were not undertaken by avowed opponents to grades and to the GPA, but either by neutral observers (Hoyt, Nelson, Cohen) or by Baird (who had a fellowship at Educational Testing Service when he wrote the review)—was that in no case was the average correlation between GPA and adult achievement (however measured) higher than .20, although it did drop as low as .09. The general range of values, based on a 95 percent confidence interval, never went higher than .31 and got as low as -.03. The overall conclusion must be that when a great many correlations produced by a great many different individuals, at many different time periods and involving a great many different criteria, are examined together, correlations between GPAs and future achievement are just not impressive. Although there are some statistical problems involved in interpreting the meaning of these correlations (for example, most correlations deal with a restricted range of grade scores, a situation that reduces correlations), the overall conclusion must be that grades do not do a very good job of predicting future adjustment or success.

Parents react in predictable ways to good and bad grades. As might be expected, how frequently parents react to both good and bad grades changes from elementary school through college. What may be surprising, however, is that reactions to grades show little or no association with good grades, and that certain reactions to bad grades actually show a negative relationship (Milton, Pollio, and Eison, 1986; Pollio, Humphreys, and Milton, 1987). There are complex problems involved in providing an unequivocal (or any) interpretation for the negative correlations observed between parental reactions and grades. The best interpretation seems to be that parents get angry at poor grades across all levels of the educational system, and this reaction does nothing to change things; if anything, it keeps things going in the same direction. Parental reactions neither cause nor ameliorate bad grades; they simply covary with them. There may well be important psychological reasons for parental reactions to grades, and a family's valuation of grades clearly plays a significant role in shaping a child's attitudes toward them. In terms of altering the grades a student receives, however, parental reactions are at best insignificant and possibly even detrimental to improving grades. Grading remains rooted in the individual classroom.

An analysis of parental reactions to both good and bad grades reveals that bad grades provoke many parents to sarcasm or anger, whereas good grades spark pride and rewards. One possible reason for these powerful reactions is that grades are viewed not only as an evaluation of academic performance but also, and more important, as a measure of one's adequacy as a parent or as indicating that one's child might not be smart enough, hardworking enough, or able to cope with personal stress. Parents worry about the future success of their children, and the meanings usually associated with grades cut a wide path across basic aspects of being a "good" parent and of having a "good" child. Parental reactions seem more pertinent to the needs of parents than to those of students or of teaching and learning.

Attention to the use made of grades by business recruiters and to parental reactions simply reinforces the fundamental observation that grades, primarily and essentially, must be used as a mode of communication between teachers and students in the specific learning situations defined by distinct courses. The proper context for grades is also the basic context for learning; grades thus should be employed in ways that facilitate significant learning, as suggested in the following recommendations.

Recommendations

Most faculty are averse to tilting at windmills, and most perceive grades and grading (and GPAs) as so ingrained in university life that little can be done to correct abuses. Yet we also believe that some things can be done to improve the legitimate use of grades and grading in a specific classroom as a communication between teacher and student, so as to facilitate teaching and learning. Sustained and thoughtful faculty discussion of grading in relation to testing and course requirements is important—but not to bring uniformity to our practices or to coerce colleagues into procedures antithetical to their values. Rather, attention to these issues brings greater clarity to classroom values and procedures; suggests new approaches to grading, teaching, learning, and testing; and promotes a greater collegial understanding of these matters as students experience them in specific individual classes.

The context in which grades are meaningfully given, received, and used is the individual course or class. Within this context, grades are best used as a communication between an instructor and a student. When we perceive grades as part of a complex process of communication, we recognize that they can be used to facilitate learning. Faculty should clarify, individually and collegially, their understanding of grades, with this as their primary emphasis. They should not encourage the use too often made of these symbols: to rank and sort students for other institutional and societal purposes.

Instructors should integrate the basic criteria and procedures for grading into their approaches to teaching and learning. Grading should flow from course objectives and instructional strategies, not vice versa. An instructor's grading system and procedures should be coherent and, above all, apparent to the student from the outset of a course. This is not simply to allow students enmeshed in the grading game to escape being caught off base and tagged out, but to ensure that the terms of communication are clear and their relevance to what will be asked of students apparent. Grading procedures, and the tests and assignments on which they are based, must be tied to some overall logic of the course and the instructional strategies designed to implement it. If the instructor wants to promote higher orders of critical and creative thinking, and if the necessary risk taking that goes with such activities is valued, then tests and course requirements must allow and even demand these activities.

Since grades are based on classroom tests, special attention should be given to improving tests. Our tests define our academic values in ways that transcend all that we say in our opening monologues or in our course syllabi. Improving tests entails reflection, practice, and skill, as well as critiques by colleagues at times, especially if we are to design questions and activities that involve students in higher levels of critical and creative thinking. Feedback to students on tests and other assignments should contain more than the simple notation of a grade or indications of what is right or wrong. A test is not only a grading device but also a teaching technique in its own right (Milton, 1982).

We must recognize that grades are judgments made by human beings about complex processes. As judgments, they are necessarily subjective. This does not mean that they are capricious or arbitrary; it does mean that they are made in specific contexts, and that these contexts are shaped by a number of factors, ranging from the social characteristics and values of a specific historical era to the priorities and perceptions of individual students and teachers. Grades are human judgments about a complex human phenomenon; they cannot always be quantified or expressed with the exacting precision of a number taken to the second decimal. As grades, we must not idolize numerical quantification, nor should we reify too-fine distinctions not supported by the evidence on which they are supposedly based.

Each instructor should consider the number of units used in the grading scale. Just because institutions allow a five-, thirteen-, or hundred-unit scale does not mean we must use all categories on the scale. If our concern is to communicate to students our perceptions of what they know, rather than to place them in rank order, then fewer units may well serve most faculty. The grading scale should be no more finely calibrated than the information that shapes an instructor's judgments about student learning will allow.

Criteria and procedures should be fairly applied. It is striking how often students cite matters of grading as examples of unfair treatment. Nowhere is the power that resides in the hands of faculty so apparent, or so open to abuse. Some problems may be based in misperceptions of just what factors count in the eyes of a given instructor. Whether and how often one is willing to take account of so-called extraneous factors in determining grades is a matter for each instructor to decide, both in his or her own mind and in communication with students. If late papers simply will not be accepted or always will receive a penalty, this policy should be specified, for students have other instructors whose policies are different. It should go without saying—yet student anecdotal evidence indicates that this is not always the case—that factors such as gender and race must not enter into grading.

If our emphasis is helping students learn and demonstrate learning, we can avoid grading on a curve. To treat each class as a clear sample of some whole, and to accept the task of ranking and sorting as central to the classroom, forces instructors to assume adversarial positions against students and to distort testing and other evaluation procedures. We can recognize that all are not equally gifted and still make a fundamental attempt to bring all students in a class to certifiable levels of mastery. This is not a call for awarding all students A's; we simply suggest recognizing that each class is a complex entity, and assessment within it need not genuflect to external institutional and societal needs.

Faculty should seek appropriate information and avoid absolutizing grades. Faculty members often serve on all sorts of committees that make judgments about students on the basis of academic records for admission to college, specific programs, graduate and professional school; for financial aid; for academic probation or honors; and for other ends. In so doing, faculty should avoid taking out of context and removing the factors that provided their meaning. Above all, we should be wary of the GPA—a falsely precise statistic that launders grades by removing all contextual meaning, reifies grades by attributing to them properties they cannot have, and absolutizes grades by assuming they convey clear and uniform meanings. Decisions about admissions, financial aid, progress, and honors must be made, and faculty should play a significant role in making them. Therefore, we must give careful thought to the basis on which we make these decisions. We must not allow our reflections on grading and our uses of grades to be governed by sorting and ranking procedures, which are all too often at odds with grades as tools to facilitate teaching and learning through effective communication between instructors and students. We must learn to make judgments and stop relying on the GPA to take the responsibility for such judgments out of our hands.

References

Baird, L. L. "Do Grades and Tests Predict Adult Accomplishment?" *Research in Higher Education*, 1985, *23*, 3–85.

Balch, J. "The Influence of the Evaluating Instruments on Students' Learning." *American Educational Research Journal*, 1964, *1*, 169–182.

Barnett, D. C., and Dalton, J. "Why College Students Cheat." *Journal of College Student Personnel*, 1981, *22*, 545–551.

Class, E. "The Effect of the Kind of Test Announced on Students' Preparation." *Journal of Educational Research*, 1935, *28*, 358–361.

Cohen, P. A. "College Grades and Adult Achievement." *Research in Higher Education*, 1984, *20*, 281–293.

Eison, J. A., Pollio, H. R., and Cunningham, P. "Testing Preferences of Learning- and Grade-Oriented University Students." *Teaching of Psychology*, in press.

Eison, J. A., Pollio, H. R., and Milton, O. "Educational and Personal Characteristics of Four Different Types of Learning- and Grade-Oriented Students." *Contemporary Educational Psychology*, 1986, *11*, 54–67.

Hakstian, R. "The Effects of Type of Examination Anticipated on Test Preparation and Performance." *Journal of Educational Research*, 1971, *64*, 319–324.

Hoyt, D. P. *The Relationship Between College Grades and Adult Achievement: A Review of the Literature.* ACT Research Report 7. Iowa City, Iowa: American College Testing Program, 1965.

Milton, O. *Will That Be on the Final?* Springfield, Ill.: Thomas, 1982.

Milton, O., Pollio, H. R., and Eison, J. A. *Making Sense of College Grades: Why the Grading System Does Not Work and What Can Be Done About It.* San Francisco: Jossey-Bass, 1986.

Nelson, A. M. *Undergraduate Academic Achievement as an Indication of Success.* Washington, D.C.: Civil Service Commission Report, 1975.

Pollio, H. R. "What Students Think About and Do in College Lecture Classes." *Teaching-Learning Issues*, 1984, *53*, 3–18.

Pollio, H. R., Humphreys, W. L., and Milton, O. *Components of Contemporary Grade Meanings.* Technical Report No. 4. Learning Research Center, University of Tennessee, Knoxville, 1987.

Howard R. Pollio is distinguished service professor in the Department of Psychology and research associate at the Learning Research Center at the University of Tennessee, Knoxville.

W. Lee Humphreys is director of the Learning Research Center and professor in the Department of Religious Studies at the University of Tennessee, Knoxville.

Assessment will improve learning as faculty become meaningfully involved in identifying objectives and setting and communicating standards of performance.

A Synthesis with Further Recommendations

James H. McMillan

Each author in this volume has identified principles and practical examples that faculty and administrators can use to improve the assessment of student learning. As individual faculty members improve their assessments of students, the quality of teaching and learning will be enhanced. We hope that we have presented useful ideas and insights in this volume, and that at the very least it will stimulate thinking and discussion about assessing student learning. These comments synthesize the previous chapters, discuss important themes, relate these themes to institutional assessment, and suggest further reading.

Perhaps the clearest message of these chapters is that faculty need to specify the skills and knowledge they expect of students as an essential departure point for effective assessment. This theme is repeated by each author. Good instruction requires that faculty communicate their learning objectives to students. Why is this seemingly obvious step stressed by the authors? This is a first step in effective teaching, learning, and assessment, whether for individual courses or for an institution as a whole. Still, many faculty simply do not clarify their objectives, or they fail to explain what students are to learn. Some faculty play a kind of game concerning assessment and learning. The game is to keep students guessing about what will be on the test. The professor wins when students

J. H. McMillan (ed.). *Assessing Students' Learning.*
New Directions for Teaching and Learning, no. 34. San Francisco: Jossey-Bass, Summer 1988.

cannot figure out what to learn. Some faculty tell students to "know everything." Students realize that not everything can be assessed, and so they either learn some things well or many things not so well. In either case, learning is not promoted. Inferences about students' performance that are made on the basis of assessments are valid or invalid to the extent that course content is adequately sampled on tests and the curriculum and instruction are appropriate to the objectives of learning.

Another theme among the chapters is the need to establish criteria or standards to guide assessment. There is no way to remove professional judgment of students' performance. Is 90 percent or 95 percent an A? What is a B paper? What makes an excellent presentation? How many test items must you have correct to be judged competent? These questions require the professional judgment of faculty. Because each faculty member's judgments are different, students need to know the standards in operation for each class. I do this by giving students copies of papers submitted by former students, with my comments and grades. Others give practice tests, with established benchmarks. Establishing criteria is not easy; sometimes it is hard to explain what constitutes a judgment of excellence. It is especially difficult for faculty to agree on standards, and it can take a lot of time. But how else will students know how they are doing? Feedback in the form of "good," "average," or a letter grade by itself is not sufficient. Students ask what these mean, and faculty should articulate how they interpret results according to the standards they have applied to students' work (see Sadler, 1983, and McMillan, in press, for further discussion of standards and criteria as part of the professional judgment needed in assessment).

A third theme that emerges from the volume is that there are many ways to assess students' learning. While there are certain advantages in using multiple-choice tests and objectively scored surveys, there may be a tendency—especially now, with external pressures to increase assessment—to use them too much. Faculty need to be careful not to allow the method of assessment to drive what is and is not assessed. Assessment techniques should be identified after the objectives and purposes of an assessment are well defined. In other words, don't put the means before the ends. It is better, given limited resources, to conduct effective small-scale assessments rather than weak large-scale evaluations. Often the most appropriate type of assessment is a qualitative one, or a combination of quantitative data gathering, interviews, and observations of performance. For example, in my institution I am involved in an effort to identify and assess student values. One approach would have been to administer existing, standardized value surveys, but there was little correspondence between our assessment objectives and the content of the surveys. Furthermore, we needed information for two particular purposes: to identify discrepancies between student and institutional values, and to ascertain institutional influences on values. One qualitative technique we are piloting, which seems appropriate, is focus group interviewing. This technique, used extensively in marketing research, provides the quality and richness of information needed in researching an area like values (Hambrick, 1987). Briefly, it involves a semistructured interview of a group of eight to ten students. A trained interviewer asks questions and facilitates discussion to create a synergistic environment in which the students are stimulated by others and by the discussion. We are also exploring the use of written responses to case studies that involve ethical dilemmas.

One more theme deserves some attention. It is clear that improving assessment is hard work and requires an investment of time and energy. Faculty simply need to become more involved in assessment. Involvement will increase as faculty need to come to agreement about course and program goals and criteria for judging performance. One of the most stimulating and helpful faculty activities is discussion and debate about what should be taught and how it should be judged. Institutionwide assessment needs faculty involvement as well. To involve faculty is to engage them meaningfully. Faculty participation is usually sought in assessment programs, but too often in a way that does not directly affect or interest faculty. Also, as Loacker points out in Chapter Two, institutional policies for promotion, tenure, and merit increases need to reflect the role of assessment in effective teaching. Department chairs, deans, and provosts are in positions to implement reward structures that emphasize assessment focused on improved student learning.

The literature on assessment seems to be divided into three categories. The first focuses on principles and on issues of constructing, administering, and evaluating tests that faculty give in classrooms. Jon F. Wergin, at the end of Chapter One, summarizes additional resources in this area. The second category includes assessment related to a specific aspect of the curriculum. The chapters on critical thinking, writing, experiential learning, and assessing the major cite important resources and additional references. The third category concerns the recent emphasis on what I term *accountability assessment,* a focus on institutionwide student outcomes. The best source of current information for the third category is the American Association for Higher Education Assessment Forum, directed by Pat Hutchins. This group monitors assessment activities across the country and provides resources and services related to assessment, including an annual conference, commissioned papers, access to unpublished reports, a national directory of programs, and a network of professionals working in assessment. Materials from the Assessment Forum are available through the ERIC system using the identifier "AAHE Assessment Forum." Several good sources provide an introduction to institutional assessment, including Adelman (1986), Banta (in

102

press), Bray and Belcher (1987), Ewell (1983, 1985), Halpern (1987), and *Change* (1987).

This volume began with a message from Cross (1987), and it ends with another from the same source: "Our national goal to improve the quality of undergraduate education necessarily starts in the classroom" (p. 7). We hope we have been successful in presenting theory, principles, experience, and recommendations that will improve student learning through effective assessment.

References

Adelman, C. (ed.). *Assessment in American Higher Education: Issues and Context.* Office of Educational Research and Improvement. U.S. Department of Education, 1986.

Banta, T. W. (ed.). *Educational Outcomes Assessment: Promise and Perils.* New Directions for Institutional Research, no. 59. San Francisco: Jossey-Bass, in press.

Bray, D., and Belcher, M. (eds.). *Issues in Student Assessment.* New Directions for Community College, no. 59. San Francisco: Jossey-Bass, 1987.

Change, January/February 1987 (entire issue).

Ewell, P. T. *Information on Student Outcomes: How to Get It and How to Use It.* Boulder, Colo.: National Center for Higher Education Management Systems, 1983.

Ewell, P. T. (ed.). *Assessing Educational Outcomes.* New Directions for Institutional Research, no. 47. San Francisco: Jossey-Bass, 1985.

Halpern, D. (ed.). *Student Outcomes Assessment: What Institutions Stand to Gain.* New Directions for Higher Education, no. 59. San Francisco: Jossey-Bass, 1987.

Hambrick, R. S. *Analysis for Decision-Making: Using Non-Quantitative Group Methods.* Richmond: School of Community and Public Affairs, Virginia Commonwealth University, 1987.

McMillan, J. H. "Beyond Value-Added Education: Improvement Alone is Not Enough." *Journal of Higher Education,* in press.

Sadler, D. R. "Evaluation and the Improvement of Academic Learning." *Journal of Higher Education,* 1983, *54* (1), 60–79.

James H. McMillan is associate professor of educational studies at Virginia Commonwealth University in Richmond. His interests are the development of critical thinking and values in college students and the assessment of educational outcomes.

Index